JUST
CLOSE IT!

Ask and You Shall Receive...

GEORGE DANS

ISBN-13: 978-0-9891618-0-0

www.TheWorldsGreatestCloser.com

BOOK DESIGN: AuthorSupport.com

CONTENTS

Introduction 1

CHAPTER ONE: *Getting You Ready to Sell* 9

CHAPTER TWO: *Attitude* 21

CHAPTER THREE: *Preparation* 31

CHAPTER FOUR: *Why Salespeople Fail* 53

CHAPTER FIVE: *What Can Be Done About It?* 61

CHAPTER SIX: *The Basics—Be a Salesperson in Control* 67

CHAPTER SEVEN: *The Sales Process—The Way to Success* 79

CHAPTER EIGHT: *Change, Adjust, and Manage* 105

CHAPTER NINE: *Objections, and What to do About Them* 115

CHAPTER TEN: *How to Let it Go and Move On* 133

CHAPTER ELEVEN: *Close the Deal* 139

CHAPTER TWELVE: *Working Toward Career Goals* 151

CHAPTER THIRTEEN: *World's Greatest Closer's Tips* 185

CHAPTER FOURTEEN: *Now What Do I Do?*. 191

APPENDIX: *Acronyms*. 197

INTRODUCTION

You picked up this book for one reason and that is to close more sales *right now*. If so, then take the book over and pay for it now. Are you going to pay cash or charge it? If you don't ask for the order, you will lose that sale, as well as all the other sales you never asked for. Just ask for the order!

If you don't close you lose, if you aren't closing you are losing, and if you aren't a closer then you are a loser. Now, that is somewhat brutal, and I hope I don't offend you. However, you bought this book because you want to become the world's best closer—am I right?

Nobody wants to be a loser. You picked up this book because you have a burning desire to be a closer. Closing is an art that has been lost due to the pressures of downsizing, cost cutting, and loss of business. You are going to discover in this book how to close any sale anytime, anyplace, and with anyone. The purpose of this book is far greater than you can imagine. If you are in sales then you were born to close, not to lose. The truth is that if you got this far, you are a winner. This book was written by the World's Greatest Closer, who is going to share with you tips and truths on how you can become a closing champion.

There aren't any secrets to closing. If you are looking for closing tricks, I don't have any. If you are looking for a silver bullet, the werewolf took it. I don't have any silver bullets, but what I do have are the best tips for you on how to become a closing champion. and it doesn't matter what you sell. Everyone is a salesperson to a degree. You are selling your kids, when

1

you tell them to clean their room; you are selling kids in sports, when you want them to give their best. You are selling if you are a manager or a coach, and you close your sale when you get people to do what you want them to do. When you were a baby, you closed your parents when you cried and they picked you up and fed you. You close the sale when you get someone to say yes to you or to buy something from you.

You close the sale when you signal someone to go first at a stop sign. You are closing every day. You close the moment you wake up and get out of bed; that in itself is a sale. When you go to church, your pastor is closing. They are closing you on believing in something that you can't see yet have heard for most of your life. That is called faith. Now talk about a tough sale, selling something you can't see or touch!

To become a closing champion is a journey that has a starting point called faith. With it, you can close anybody. With faith in yourself, your product, the company you represent, you will never be a loser. Faith is the starting point.

To be a great salesperson you have to love what you do. If you love what you do, then you do what you love, and in sales it's helping people solve their problems by providing them with solutions. Once you can solve a person's problems and show them that they can't live without what you sell, they will buy from you.

Selling is fun and exciting, and I will show you the best methods for selling. I have learned these methods through years of research and experience. I have interviewed countless top people in sales and other careers and have learned what makes them successful. Why wait for years to become the great closer? In this book you will learn how to be that great closer who will close anybody, anywhere. Will it work all the time? No. If it worked one out of four times, it would be worth it, wouldn't it? That would be a 25% closing ratio. You might be thinking, well, those aren't good odds. Actually they are; remember, most profes-sional baseball players end up in the Hall of Fame by being more of a

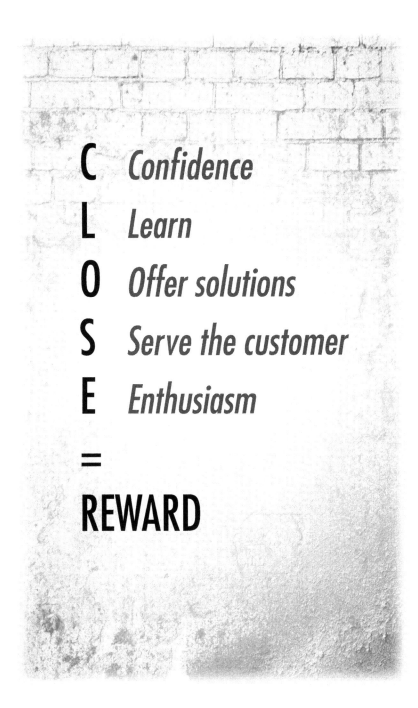

C *Confidence*

L *Learn*

O *Offer solutions*

S *Serve the customer*

E *Enthusiasm*

=

REWARD

failure than a winner. A batting average of 300 gets you into the Hall. As that great closer, you may do better than that.

However, if you are willing to pay the price for success—commitment, practice, effort, and bit of hard work—you can become the champion closer. If you are looking for a low-investment, high-return way to becoming the champion closer, then buy a lottery ticket. It's the only place you can spend a buck and make a million. This book will show you how, if you give it a chance to work for you. It's one of those books that will have an eternal shelf life and is a go-to book when you need help now or later on in your career.

Sales is fraught with failure, and soon the repeated failures take their toll. Somewhere in this book you are going to find the answer to what you need to do to close more sales. I know it's in here and you will stumble upon it almost innocently. You will see it and say, "Oh that's weird—it can't be that easy, can it? Wait a minute, there's no way that can be true, I don't believe it, can't be." It can be if you think it can be.

I found mine when I was thirty-six years old. It took me that long. I have read well over 6000 books, heard more self-help programs, attended motivational conferences, gotten advice, bought tapes, CDs, DVDs, books on quotes, and anything that had to do with finding out how to be better than I was. I found it and I moved on and *that is how* I got to where I am today. Once you find it, you will be able to do the same thing. I will save you years of looking, tons of money that you don't need to spend, and the most important thing of all, time. Life will give you but one chance. Maybe today is the day you quit putting life on layaway. Maybe you have been struggling to move forward in your personal and professional life. This book has selling skills, closing skills, but it also focuses on you, the person. The world's greatest closer's greatest close is to get you to do what you haven't been able to do yet, or have failed at.

I have trained thousands and thousands of salespeople, and during my seminars, people ask me the same question over and over: "What is your secret?"

I don't have a secret, but I do one more thing than most salespeople. I *ask* for the order or the sale. If you want to close more deals, just *ask* for the order and don't let fear stop you. If you just do that, you'll close more sales right now. The word ASK has a few different meanings:

A – S – K — ALWAYS SEEK KNOWLEDGE
A – S – K — ALWAYS SEEK KASH

It's almost biblical isn't it? The greatest self-help book in the world is called *The Best Information Before Leaving Earth* and it states in Matthew 7:7, "Ask and you shall receive!" You have to ask for the order. Just ask for it, just have the guts to ask, just develop the skills to ask for it. Just ask for it! The worst word you will ever hear is the word *no*, which means not yet. You can't let this word talk you out of asking for the sale.

How I Became The FNG- Fabulous New Guy

I remember the first time I was working in a new sales position. It was my first day on the job, and basically they threw me out on the sales floor and said, "Go get 'em, Tiger. Show us what you can do." Most companies today, they throw you out there and say, "I hope you survive and make it." Some companies show you some old dusty videos about how to sell their product. Today they tell you to go online and watch some videos on how to sell our product. No wonder there is a living graveyard with salespeople wandering around aimlessly wondering why they didn't make it in sales. I have always wanted to know how a salesperson can make it without any real-world training. How can companies expect salespeople to make quota if they aren't properly trained? No wonder there is a high turnover rate in the sales industry. You know two things happen when a salesperson leaves their job. They were either fired or they quit.

I showed up on my first day earlier than most, hoping to meet my new teammates. I got there an hour early to get prepared to sell. I was the only person there. I saw a prospect out on the showroom floor and I greeted them as best as I could. I really didn't know the company's processes but I knew what I was supposed to do: sell and close deals. And so I did. I closed the very first customer I ever talked to. Done, closed—sold. Closing and losing are black and white, yes or no. Of course when all the veterans showed up, they were somewhat mad at me. I'm not sure why. One of the old timers got real mad at me, too. He took offense at the FNG selling something. I got into an argument with this salesperson. He wanted to make sure I wasn't taking his customer. In time I became his manager and we worked it out. I helped him in many ways.

Life is too short to hold grudges. You have to let them go and focus on what is important and let go of what isn't. I was doing consulting for a company that had a top salesperson who lost that position because of his attitude. The company hired a younger salesperson who was a PhD, which means, Poor—Hungry—Driven to succeed. The veteran salesperson took a pay cut, and by that I mean his sales went down 50% because he spent more time complaining about the FNG than he did selling. It cost him thousands to worry about something that he had no control over.

I knew why I was hired. I was paid to sell. I wasn't paid to kill time, I wasn't paid to make the coffee, I wasn't paid to waste time. I wasn't paid to figure out what's for lunch or go get lunch. I was paid to close. I can remember the veterans all saying that I was the world's luckiest man. They were right; the harder I worked the luckier I got. I wasn't lucky, I knew how to close the deal and soon you will know, too.

"The person who can decide cannot be stopped, the person who hasn't decided cannot start."
— Unknown Author

ASK AND YOU SHALL RECEIVE!

CHAPTER ONE

Getting You Ready to Sell

Let's get you off the *have-to* train and get you to jump on the *get-to* train.

The biggest close of the day is closing yourself to have a great day. The moment I jump out of bed, I go into my mantra. I start it off by saying this:

> Thank God I get to get up, I'm pumped up, fired up, not giving up, letting up, or shutting up until God brings me up, I am better than most, not as good as some, but for the most part I am doing good and getting better as the day goes on. You know I had the biggest surprise today—go ahead and ask me, what was it?

> God said, "Get up, and don't ever give up, let up, or shut up until the day is up, you see with 86000 seconds in the day and 1440 minutes in the day, it's going to be hard to have a bad day. You see your problem isn't your problems, it's what your problems do to you. And for the most part that's called your

attitude; don't let the situation affect your attitude, let your attitude affect the situation. Don't tell me you're burned out because you have never been on fire, and if you aren't fired up with enthusiasm—no problem—I will fire you up with enthusiasm. Now go get fired up."

I say that mantra everyday and if you ever meet me, ask me how I am feeling and get ready to hear it.

Too often people wake up and say, "Oh, I have to go to work, I have to make money, I have to sell something or I am going to get fired, I have to get to work on time, I have to be in traffic." You know at some time you have to get off the *have-to* train and get on the *get-to* train. So do you rise and shine or do you rise and whine? It's a choice, isn't it? I had a person once ask me, "Do you wake up grouchy?" I responded with, "No I wouldn't touch her with a ten foot pole." Anyway, life is mostly mental, and so is selling.

Jump out of bed today instead of crawling out of bed. Get up before the alarm goes off and don't hit the snooze button, because you will be behind all day. So often people complain about how hard life is instead of appreciating how good life is. That is a close right there. Be happy you woke up today, at least you get to go and you get to have the day today. Have you ever caught yourself saying, "Life isn't fair?" I can tell you this: if you are fair to life, it will be fair to you. Give a little and expect a little. Give it everything you have and you will have everything you need.

People like you understand the need to always be on the self-improvement train. You understand that to have progress in life, you must become transparent. That means being truthful with yourself. Do it quickly and you will get more out of this book than you can imagine. Life is so short that before you know it, you turn around and you have lost the pep in your step. Now you need to take pep so you can step. Life is fleeting—you only have one, and it would be a shame to waste it. Life is nothing more than a race to the end. Why would you hold out?

What would you do if you knew you only had so much time for living? You would go for it, wouldn't you?

What about tomorrow? It will never be here today. Yesterday will never come back, so why not do it now? Why do people put life on layaway? Why are they always looking for something better? Why don't they just seize the moment now? Don't wait! Quit talking and start doing. You will be amazed at how much further you will get if you jump into action. "Yeah, but—" Yeah, but what? "I'm not sure the timing is right." Whatever! Get going now, not later, or you will find yourself someday as an old fool nodding wisely but speaking stupidly, saying, I shoulda, coulda, woulda. Too late—GOYA (Get Off Your Ass!) and get going!

How Do I Get The Most Out Of This Book?

Read it over and over until you recognize where you can improve yourself and your skills. You might want to get a highlighter and when something hits you, then either highlight it or circle it. Whatever you do, don't be so careful of the book that you don't mark it up or earmark a page when something hits you between your eyes.

Two kinds of people buy books. One reads the first or second chapter and then places the book on a shelf. The other reads it, learns from it, and applies the principles. The *shelf-help* person puts life on layaway and won't buy another book until they knock the dust off their shelf-help book. The *self-help* person is a student of life and their profession. That is you!

How did you get this book?

Did you purchase it, download it, or was it given to you? It really doesn't matter. What really matters is what you are going to do now that you

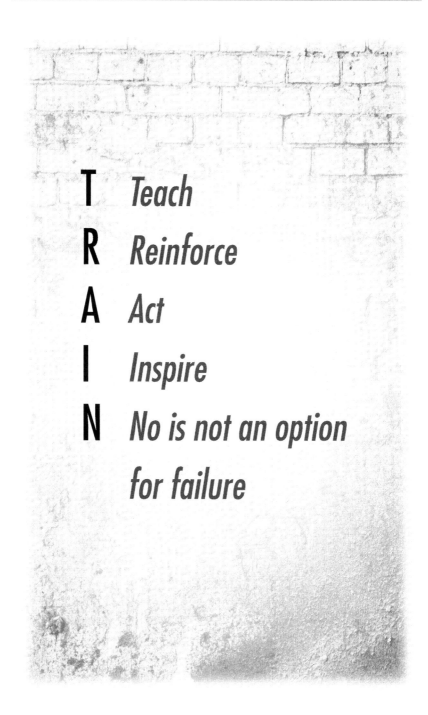

T *Teach*

R *Reinforce*

A *Act*

I *Inspire*

N *No is not an option*

for failure

have it. Today is a new day for you, and that means that whatever happened before doesn't really apply to today. Think of it like a blackboard in school—you can take out the eraser today and wipe it clean. The board is clean and uncluttered, which will allow you to focus on what you are going to get out of this book. It is so hard to go forward while looking backward, isn't it? Why do you think the rearview mirror is so small while the windshield is huge? The world is ahead of you, not behind you. Life wants you to be successful. You owe it to yourself, your family, your company, and your customers. It doesn't matter where you have been; it only matters where you are going. If you have any luggage you need to get rid of, drop it off today; it's hard to go forward by carrying your past. Let it go so you can prepare to become the Champion Closer. Come on this journey with me and learn from the best on how to close more sales. I will be with you the entire way encouraging you, selling you, and finally closing you to give everything you have to becoming the best person and closer. Everybody has potential but so many people are so proud of it that they never use it.

Don't wait for someday!

Someday will never be here. Someday is not a day in the week. People have all kinds of rules that they live by, and maybe you have some too. People say, "Now is not the time to do this, I can get to that later, this won't work for me," I have already heard this before, "It has a nice cover, that's why I bought the book." Covers do sell books, however it's the words that are powerful and when you learn how to articulate the words, you will close more sales. Just follow through and you will be more successful in life. Why is that? Most salespeople will surrender and throw up the white flag because it takes work to change. Most of them talk a big game, but when it comes to playing, they are on the sidelines screaming like some Little League parent. Talk is cheap, isn't it? Most likely you will win by default because most people quit when the going gets tough.

There are so many salespeople who have failed at selling. Most failed because they weren't committed to their career. If you piled up the bodies of all the salespeople who tried and failed at sales, the heap would reach the moon. People will say this—maybe you have said this, "Not now, I'm going to keep my options open and see how things turn out." Have you ever said that? What are you waiting for?

Fighting Mediocrity

Why would you settle for mediocrity? You don't want to live there, and if you are there, give your notice and tell your mind that you are leaving. Life is all about giving your best, no matter where you are. Life will never deny success to the person who gives their very best in every situation. Life won't cheat you, but you will cheat it. Your paycheck will reflect your efforts. It won't lie to you. You have to believe that you have a lot to give to the world—in life and selling. If you are in sales, then you are in the business of serving people. That's your purpose: to help people solve their problems, needs, wants with something that will make them and their company more profitable. You don't want to live your life hitting average with amazing accuracy. You want go for it right now. Life will give you one run, one race, one life. Why would you hold out?

Don't let your past failures hold you back from running forward. Everybody has setbacks and if you have failed, then call it an education. At least you know what not to do, right? Do you see how you can use failure to launch you? Change is hard. I will talk about it throughout the book. Change, for most salespeople, is the enemy. Your comfort zone doesn't want you to leave it, because it will be vacant. It will fight you with every ounce of energy it has. Comfort zones don't like change.

You can't change what you tolerate.

If you tolerate mediocrity then you will stay there. The reason you will stay there is because you feed it. You actually accommodate it by living with it. You either tolerate it, eliminate it, or motivate it. Go for door number two and eliminate it. You can, if you draw a line in the sand. That means you will do whatever it takes to fight mediocrity without sacrificing your morals. You can purchase a one-way ticket called freedom. Talk won't get you there, but action will. You have to be willing to fight for whatever you desire in life and work. There will be times when you will get knocked down, knocked out. Nobody cares about you being knocked out, but they do care if you get back up.

Every person has it in them; all you need to do it tap into it. You have the drive inside of you to do this. Think about what you would go through if you were starving. You would do just about anything to eat, wouldn't you? You have the drive inside you already. All you have to do is transfer that hunger drive over to your sales career.

Go to war with faith, effort, and belief in self—the Closer's armor.

The world's greatest closer has an armor that is fortified with faith, effort, and belief in self. Be willing to fight for what you desire in life and your career, and you will end up as the victor. Take a stand today and press on, go around, go under, go over, move aside the past, your old ways, old habits, and old failures to reach your goals. You can have all the enthusiasm you want but it will only carry you so far.

How many times have you seen a new salesperson come into your business and jump to the top of the sales board? How can that be? How can a new salesperson literally fly by the veterans who have been there for years? Have you ever seen it happen? You are almost jealous, aren't you? Of course you would never admit it but it does happen, doesn't it?

After a while, wonder boy or wonder girl comes back down to reality, don't they? It happens because the *nos* start to affect their thinking and soon they lose their enthusiasm and confidence. I personally have been the FNG many times; however, I avoided the ninety-day wonder-boy label. You can do the same if your skills match your enthusiasm. You have to back your enthusiasm with skills so that you can maintain your success and overcome your failures. I know if you put, faith, effort, and belief together you can't be stopped. I know; I am living proof. My words aren't hollow.

How did you get in and will you be able to stick it out?

For the most part people fall into sales by default when other jobs or careers end or don't work out. The reason for this is that most of the time you don't need a degree to get a job in sales. There are always openings for salespeople. Pick up the newspaper and you will see ads for sales; go online and you will see sales ads posted on numerous websites. What about you? How did you get in sales? Maybe you had a forced

career change, you were fired or your company had cutbacks, downsizing, or you got tired of what you were doing and decided to quit. I like sales because it's one of the few careers that you can get in without a degree—often with little or no experience.

How exciting! I don't have to go to college to be a salesperson. I can show up with pep in my step and bit of gleam in my eye and tell them I can sell anything. Okay, it might be a bit more than that; however, you can get in with a little down. I don't know where you are in your life or where you are going. You might be in a bookstore or on the net looking for information on how to sell and close. Maybe you just closed your family business, got laid off, quit your job, got fired from a job, weren't making enough money, or had enough of somebody always telling you what to do. I can help you out right here, if you are coming in, jump in, don't test the water to see if it's cold. Jump in and get going.

How many sales jobs have you had?

Salespeople for the most part are nomadic. It seems like they go on tour like a rock star. They go from job to job, city to city, and soon they come back to where they started. I have seen it at so many of the trade shows I have attended. Same faces, same suits, just a different name tag and product. People leave their jobs because they are asked to leave, don't believe in their product anymore, their company was downsizing, the products are out dated, or their heart wasn't in what they were selling, and they needed a break from sales. What about you?

Prepare Like A Selling Champion — Speak And Grow Rich

Selling really isn't a physical sport but more of a mental sport, and like any great athlete you need to prepare yourself the right way. If you don't, then you will lose sales and more important, you will lose money and your attitude. They key to the vault of success is being prepared to go to the game of selling and win. The biggest tool you have is your mouth, and the worst thing you could do is start selling without warming up your vocabulary. No world-class athlete would just show up and dress up and say, "Let's go get 'em," would they?

With sales being competitive, proper preparation is important to your success. Salespeople spend far too much time working in their business instead of working on their business; you have to do the opposite thing for yourself. When in doubt sell yourself with hard work and effort, and you won't be stopped. Warm up and you won't throw up.

Why the word *Why* is a hidden killer

"Why can't I sell more? Why can't I be at the top of the selling board? Why can't I do better? Why does this always happen to me? Why does that person seemingly get all the right customers? Why didn't I get that job promotion? Why don't I make more money? Why is that nothing good ever happens to me? Why can't I get myself together? Why can't I get what I deserve?"

People ask those questions and certain feelings come up. When things aren't going well, we look for answers and they seemingly can't be found. Guess what—you don't have to look any farther then the bathroom mirror! The answer is right there. Your search is over. Look hard at the person in the mirror. When you come to the truth, the pains of life will be less. Why can't you just tell the truth? It's hard to face reality, isn't it? Most people would rather run from it than run to it.

I ask people, what is your closing ratio? For the most, I get some foggy wishy-washy answer. The only way to improve your closing ratio is to know your numbers. Who cares if your closing ratio is 5% or 10%, what matters is that you know it so you can accurately put a plan together to improve it. I can't even begin to count how many times I

J *Just*

O *Over*

B *broke*

A job is what you do.
Jobs don't have a future,
Careers do.

have heard salespeople say, buyers are liars. Yes, but so are salespeople when they play hide and seek with their numbers.

No Is My Enemy — No means not yet!

Your enemy is the word *no*—if it were easy to sell, everyone would be able to overcome the word no. The word no will chase you forever. If you develop and maintain your skills you can keep if from catching you and throwing you out of sales.

No doesn't mean never, it means, or can mean, *not now*. Your prospect needs to know more to say yes. Do you see how the word no has more meanings? No, for some reason, is a salesperson's worst enemy and it has destroyed many a salesperson's career and life. Why is that, you ask? It's because they never developed the skills to handle and overcome the word. Most salespeople go through their entire life never really figuring out how to overcome the word no. No means "tell me more so I can say yes." No is two thirds of yes. It needs just one more letter. No will be around the corner of success forever, and it takes skills to overcome it. Think of it like this: when you hear no, that is actually the beginning of the sale. Get your game on and get ready to overcome it—you might have to overcome it several times.

I have often wondered how many salespeople have failed because they never developed their skills to handle and overcome this two-letter powerful word. That's not you. If you picked this book up, again, it's because you want to know, "how can I learn how to overcome the nos I will face in my career as a salesperson." You cannot let the no word destroy you or your confidence. You will hear it forever, since your parents started using on you. With the right skills, I can tell you that you should be able to minimize it. It's going to follow you as long as you are in sales. No means not now, not necessarily never. You can do it, you can overcome it.

CHAPTER TWO

Attitude

World's greatest attitude

Selling is all about attitude, and your attitude is like a muscle that needs to be conditioned every day. I can prove to you that *attitude* is 100%. Go ahead and fill out the scores for what each letter is, for example A is number one, with twenty-six letters in the alphabet, Z would be number twenty-six.

A–T–T–I–T -U -D–E
1–20   TOTAL SCORE _____

H–A–R–D–W–O–R–K
8 +   NOW ADD IT UP = _____

It goes to show you that attitude is everything isn't It?

Now check out Knowledge

K–N–O–W–L–E–D–G–E
11+   TOTAL IS _____

Now take a look at the how far God will take you:

L–O–V–E–O–F–G–O–D
12+   TOTAL IS _____

All the above are important. However, there will never be anything stronger than the love of God. Hard work will bring you only so far in life, your knowledge will bring you a bit closer, and your attitude will bring you right up to the finish line. However, the love of God will bring you past your finish line and your wildest dreams. I know. I have had my share of hardships as a salesperson and as an everyday person. In all the books I have read and researched, when I stop at the intersection of where I was, where I am, and where I am going, the answers or solutions to my problems come from the love of God. Whatever a man or woman believes is their own choice. I would never sell you on the above. You can make your own choices and you will live or die with them.

Check Up From The Neck Up

Closers take time to work and develop their attitude, because they know that the word *no* will come at them quite often. Having an attitude of gratitude is very important. As I stated above, so many people are on the *have-to* train and in real life you might want to get off that train and get on the *get-to* train. You don't have to do anything in life, if you think about it. You get to: you get to wake up, you get to get to work, you get to improve. You get to determine, for the most part, how you feel about your life and work. You have the power to choose your attitude throughout most of your life. It's not what happens to you, but how you handle what happens to you.

In my seminars the first thing I start off is opening up with an attitude of gratitude. I like to remind everyone, how lucky or blessed they are to be here—able to wake up today, appreciate their families, kids, and the surroundings they have. Too often we take for granted what we have, don't we? We forget how important life is and what we already have. It seems like the business world is all about getting ahead. What about enjoying what you have?

I once heard a saying that went like this: The richest person on earth is the person who has what they want and can enjoy what they have. Maybe it's time to smell the flowers and enjoy the times you have right now. Appreciate what you have because someday you will have to give it all back and most likely you won't be ready to give it back at that time. I often wonder why so many people are unhappy where they are. When will those people be happy? Is life all about searching? I once heard a person say that the rung on the ladder wasn't meant to rest. Why not? Why can't you enjoy your successes for a short time. If you don't, then when you arrive, you will never know if this is the time to enjoy what you worked for.

. . . .

"Don't let the situation affect your attitude, let your attitude affect the situation" —Dan Wood

I Can't Let It Go—But You Have to

When a salesperson loses a sale, they often carry the negative effect all day long. If you allow that to happen, then it will cloud your vision, wreck your attitude, and affect you when you get in front of your next prospect. You can't pay attention to something that won't bear a good result. When you lose a sale, you can't brood or go around all day long moaning and whining. It's done, it's over, let it go. Learn how to say the word *next* out loud, clap your hands, and let it go. You must signal to your mind that it is over. If you don't, it will cost you money. Look at pro sports players; nobody hits 100%. Nobody bowls a perfect game every game, nobody throws a no hitter every time they pitch; as a matter of fact, baseball players fail more then they succeed. Batters fail 70% of the time and succeed only 30% of the time and that earns them a ticket to the Hall of Fame. Sales is the same way, isn't it? I know you will fail more than you succeed, but if you are of a strong mind, you will learn how to overcome the rejection and move past it. Charles Swindoll said that "life is 10% what happens to you and 90% how you handle it." Attitude is nearly everything.

Selling is the same thing. Developing a positive mental attitude takes work, and your brain is a muscle that needs to be exercised every day. Sales is all about getting more swings and getting your bat off your shoulder and swinging for the fences. Look, you can go zero for three today and get one more swing in the game, just as you can get one more chance to close a sale today. Who cares what happened and for now, why it happened? The only thing you can do right now is to get your game face on, and focus on what is right in front of you. Then swing for the fences, throw every bit of what you have left in your tank, and prove to your prospect that they can't live without you or your product. Now ASK and close your sale. You can do it!

How To Improve Attitudes

Reading books on developing a positive attitude is a vital as putting gas in your car, eating, and showering. Most people don't work on their attitude everyday, and what happens is that soon the selling losses take their toll. When a salesperson loses their positive attitude, then their selling and life faith leave them. Doubt creeps in. It's like cancer; it will eat and destroy you.

I can't tell you how many times I have heard salespeople who won't ask for the order. Why? Because they have allowed the repeated failures to steal away their confidence, enthusiasm, and positive attitude. The world's great closers have the ability to overcome repeated failures and the blows of life with faith, confidence, and professional selling skills. You can't give up, let up, or shut up until you write them up and close them up!

But But But—Get Off The But Bus

"I don't have the time." Actually you do, it's what you do with your time that controls just about everything. If you want to get more focused, then do less. One of the worst words to come about in the last twenty-five years or so is the word multitasking. People say I can do this and that, and this and that, but not much ever gets done. Every day you get one day, you should enjoy and treasure it. If you don't use all your time, then you have to give it back. Unfortunately you can't roll your minutes over like you can on a cell phone. I can tell you this though—when you get to the end of your life, you will always want more time.

. . . .

"It is far better to grow in life then just to go through life."

If you take the time to grow your life, then you can expect to grow your income. Selling is like a race, if you don't take time to stretch out, you most likely will pull a muscle. Think of your mouth and brain as muscles. As long as you have a hunger to improve you will never be able to over-stuff them.

Self-help or Shelf-help

The world's greatest closers take the time to develop themselves to be great closers. One day I was walking by the baby nursery. I didn't see a sign that said, "closers and losers." You have probably heard this one, too. "Oh, that person is a natural born salesperson." No. That is a person who has developed their skills to make selling seem natural.

 If you spend time getting dressed, then spend time getting your inside dressed. Allot time everyday to self improvement; the pay-off is great. Closers are in school for their entire life. You can normally spot them when you get in their car. They normally have self-help CDs or tapes playing, or even have books on improving themselves with them. Too often salespeople buy the books, but they end up on their bookshelves. That's why I call it shelf-help. Developing into the world's greatest closer is a process, a lifelong journey, that takes education backed with effort. Tons of people know what to do, they just can't seem to do it.

Positive Thinking

Read *The Power of Positive Thinking* was written by Dr. Norman Vincent Peale. Thinking positive will help you close more sales and lead a better life. Thinking negatively will destroy your confidence and plunge you into a darkness called worry. You will never live longer by worrying. Worry will destroy your life.

I heard a story years ago. "I used to worry so much and finally one day, I hired a person to worry for me. I pay the person $10,000 a month to worry for me." My friend came over and said, "You look so much better, what's up?" I said, "Well for one thing, I don't worry anymore. I am paying a person $10,000 a month to worry for me." My friend said, "Are you crazy? How can you afford to pay $10,000 a month for this person?" I shot back, "That's not my problem; they have to worry about that."

For the most part, selling is a game of numbers that will result in closing or losing. It's black and white. The way to develop is to work on your positive mindset, work with positive people, and think positive thoughts throughout the day. Show me a reader and I will show you a leader. Reading reinforces your thoughts, which will determine your mindset and the actions you will take. Be very careful of the words you use, because they will send signals to your subconscious mind. Just think about how many times a day you say these words: can't, maybe, if only, I wish, try, why me, life sucks, I hate this, or I should. Those words will destroy your self-esteem and self-worth. They need to be replaced with power words, such as I can, I will, I know, I'm going to. Do you recognize the difference now? You talk to yourself most of the day and are closing yourself to win or lose.

Subconscious Thinking

The subconscious part of your mind never sleeps, so if you plant weeds in your garden— your brain—don't expect roses to grow. Good in, good out, trash in, trash out. Peale said that the words you use will determine how high you set your goals. If you don't take the time to clear your mind or move past your old failures, regrets, hates, insecurities, and negative thinking, the results can be fatal to your career. They way you feel is determined by the thoughts that fill your mind. When you are a positive thinker, it's almost like you have armor and a steel-trap mind. If you take the time daily to fill your mind with positive thoughts, you will soon expel your negative thoughts and lack of confidence, along with their friend, doubt. Get back to reading or hearing positive thoughts. It is not enough to say, "Oh I say positive things all day." That is the equivalent of looking at food all day and not eating it. You can't get full by just looking at food. Reading and learning—the same thing.

Positive thinking is like hitting the human refresh button every day. With so many energy leaks and energy thieves in life, you have to take time everyday to develop your mind. Once you have emptied your mind, now you have to fill it with something. Reading or hearing positive thoughts will fill your mind with boundless energy. Too often we hear salespeople say, "I'm burned out." Who is burned out, the top-selling person or the bottom salesperson? Normally the bottom salesperson says he's burned out. How can that person be burned out? They've never been on fire!

Optimism is catchy. Is yours worth catching? The world's great closers know that optimism will help them through their downtimes. No matter how great a closer you are, failure will always be lurking

around the corner of success. They go hand in hand. If you closed everyone you met, then you probably don't need this book. Optimistic closers see opportunity in everything they do. Every opportunity is another chance for them to sell. Closers have an attitude of "I can" instead of "I can't". They say, "I will" instead of "I might." When they lose, they say, "I will get them next time." Pessimistic people always seem to look on the dark side of life. You can hear them when they say, "Yeah but that won't work, they probably won't see me, I can't get hold of them, they probably have already bought, our product is way too much money, why would they buy in a down economy."

Do you now see how your words will determine your thought process? The more optimistic you are in your approach to life and work, the better life will treat you. You have probably heard the catchy saying, "Is the glass half full or half empty?" It's always full: half water and half air. Closers can see and feel optimism no matter how bad life and work are. I know that people have dark days. I lost my brother-in-law in an armed robbery. Standing at his coffin before I said goodbye to him for the last time, was one of the hardest times of my life. My optimism meter was at an all time low, but deep down, I knew if I could get through that day, I could get through any day. I never got

JUST CLOSE IT!

over it; I only learned how to get through it, and sometimes that's all you can do in life. Everybody has setbacks. The only thing that matters is how you come back, and if you can come back.

You can get through anything if you stay optimistic. It takes work. When I was a fireman, I had to perform CPR many times, knowing that only about one out of ten live. I was optimistic that I could bring everyone back. Not once did I ever say, oh this guy or gal won't make it, so I will only give 50% today. I say why not always give 100%?

Optimistic closers say, I will never give up, let up, or shut up, until I write them up and close them up. Start repeating that saying over and over: I will never give up, let up, shut up, until I write them up and close them up. Write it down and repeat it several times a day!

CHAPTER THREE

Preparation

Five P's of Success: Proper Planning Prevents Poor Performance

Most people spend about 80% of their morning getting ready on their outside appearance and only about 20% on their inside which is their body and mind. Most likely the 20% is stopping off to get a quick bite, an energy drink, and a smoke. That's not enough to help you be the world's greatest closer. Selling is like a sport and you have to take it seriously; mental preparation and physical preparation have to be in sync. Most salespeople will tell you that they don't have the time to prepare a workout. Let me break that myth. There are 86,400 seconds in day, 1440 minutes in day, twenty-four hours in a day and on average if you work 4.5 weeks a month there are 180 work hours. Most likely you have the time, but self-help is not one of your priorities. Salespeople spend far more time wasting time than investing in time to improve. Your paycheck is your report card.

This saying, proper planning prevents poor performance, has been around for years and is used by the top performers in sales. They are driven salespeople who have a game plan for every day they work. The world's great closers preplan their month before they start it. Stephen Covey said that you must begin with the end in mind. You have to be able to visualize your goals at the beginning of the year, month, and day. You have to see it first; that is what motivates you. You have to see the rewards of your planned work first. The only way to do that is to finish your month before you start it.

Do salespeople have bad months?

Have you ever had a bad month? How about a couple of bad months? Have you ever lost a job because you had several bad months? Do salespeople have bad months or do they have bad days that, when added up, result in a bad month? Salespeople have bad months, because the bad days add up. Most likely the salesperson was not activity driven. Effort and hard work are great habits to have; however, you have to direct your effort and hard work at productive activities that will lead you to sales.

The best way to prevent a bad month is to forecast and manage your activities. Selling is like a football game, the coach finishes the game before it starts. You see the coach on the sidelines with a large laminated sheet. That sheet contains their plays and activities. The coach has to manage each play along with each player. Never would a pro coach show up at a Sunday game and say, "Hey boys, here is the ball, go get 'em." The coach knows how many plays they are going to run, pass, kick, and so on. Sales is the same way. If you want to be a wing boy or girl, I can tell you this; your sales are going to fly up. You will drown in minor activities instead of majoring in major things.

Keys to a great month

Start forecasting your activities and then manage your activities every day. That is called MTD, month to date. That means you have to know the scoreboard of your selling activities every day. If you do that, then you can minimize the chances of cramming your month in the last week of the month. Forecasting will make it easier for you to reach your sales goals. The last thing you want to do is work hard and not see results.

Forecast:

1. Phone calls
2. Mail outs
3. Emails
4. Appointments
5. In-person visits
6. Presentations of product or services
7. Demonstration of products or services
8. Cold Calls
9. Follow-up of sold customers
10. Referrals

You can do all of this in a planner or on your computer. Take time at the beginning of the month to come up with your results goal and your activity goal. Manage your activity and soon the results will be there. Each day adjust your activities so that you can prevent cramming of your month in the last week. If you get behind a bit, it's easier to adjust, if you get behind a lot, then it's hard to do a lot at the end of the month. If you preplan your month and follow it accordingly, with controlled attention and management of activities, the month will come together.

Hurry, there's a fire

When I was younger I entered the fire service because I was going to be a fireman. How often have you heard, "What's the hurry, are you going to a fire?" Several times we went to fire, and we were in a controlled hurry. Most of the time, we knew exactly what to do because of our training and practice but more than that, it was our preplanning of what to do when we got to the fire. We did a forecast of the fire, which in reality is a fire inspection. We would go out and inspect the premises and take notes. We would enter them in our planner or preplan file and review them. You never know when the bell is going to ring but when it rings, you want to make sure you have your game face on, because fighting fires is life or death. Sales is not life or death, but it might be to your paycheck or career.

No Power Without Organized Effort

It will be hard to harness your efforts without a written plan. The world's greatest closers can maintain continuous effort and activities with a plan. That is the backbone of success. Knowing exactly what you have to do to reach your results. It wasn't too long ago that I saw focus pills for sale. The vitamin for focus is called a plan. I like what T. Boone Pickens said: "A fool with a plan is better than a genius without a plan."

When is my ship coming in? Never, if you don't send it out

How often have you have heard the saying, "Someday my ship is going to come in." I can't wait and I wonder why it hasn't come in yet. You have to set the sail and send the ship out. Then you have to manage your plan so that your ship doesn't end up on the rocks. A captain sees the land only 5% of the voyage. They see it when they leave and see it when they arrive. The rest of the time, they are managing the trip plan. Not once do they set sail and say, "Let's just go the way the wind blows."

Those ships and salespeople go around in circles, never reaching their destination.

Accurate thinking develops an accurate plan

Chaos is defined as an extreme case of disorder and confusion. Once you have your month planned out, then each day you come to work, review, and adjust accordingly. Chaos will dry up like water in the desert. You will be able to have controlled attention which brings out the word focus.

F — FAITHFULLY
O — ON
C — COURSE
U — UNTIL
S — SUCCESSFUL

Know Thy Product

There is nothing worse than a salesperson who doesn't know their product. *USA Today* quoted years ago that the number one cause of death of a salesperson was due to their lack of knowledge. If you don't know your product, the results will be fatal to you as a salesperson. The negatives and the cost are heavy because you won't be able to get behind what you sell and your prospects will sense that right away. If you aren't convinced of your product, then you won't be able to get behind it and convince your prospect. If you are a professional tele-commuter and don't know your product, then most likely you will die a slow painful death. Since your prospect can't see the largest part of communication—body language—you are doomed.

One way to learn more about your product is to take time out every day to study your product and learn the best features about your product and why it is superior to your competitor's product. Then make a written list of why your product is superior to your competition. The results are fantastic. Get some flash cards and write out reasons why people would buy your product. If I were you, I would review them daily so that you are prepared to sell in any condition.

There is nothing worse than a prospect telling you, "Oh we need to compare or shop around because we don't want to make a bad decision." If you knew why your competitive advantages were better than your competition then you might have a greater chance at closing them right on the spot. Often salespeople just buy in on what their prospect says and come back with an answer like this. "Well, okay, you folks go ahead and take some time. Call me if you have any questions." That is weak. Do you think your prospects are going to go home and pop popcorn or something like that? Hardly, they just go on to the next place and buy. It happens often, doesn't it?

What happened? You didn't close the sale. Why not? You didn't do your homework, and now you pay the fine—your lost commission. Think about how many times you sold a prospect who was just at another similar business. Has that ever happened to you? Did you

 mail part of your commission to the losing salesperson? Now remember the word *closer* here. Nobody is a personal loser if they are giving their best every day.

How many times have you gone to buy something and left because the salesperson didn't know their product? The only sure way to close a prospect when you don't know your product is to drop the price. When you drop the price, then you drop your commission, the value of your product, and your income. It doesn't take any skill to drop the price, but it takes knowledge of your product and skill to hold the price.

. . . .

"It takes skills to pay the bills." —*George Dans*

Show up to work and work

What an amazing concept—*work*. If you don't have your day planned out, then it plans you out, and before you know it the day is over—and soon the month and your job. The world's greatest closers have their day planned out the day before so that when they get to work they work.

Give your best today—Life will not deny you success if you give your best every day.

If you give less than your best, then that means you are giving your worst. The world's greatest closers sets their standards high and then do everything they can to reach those standards. Your standards will never fail you but you may fail to reach your standards. I have said for years in my seminars and private workshops that those who aim for average will hit it with amazing accuracy. You don't need permission to be mediocre in life. Hell, you can just show up and waste time, and some companies are okay with that. As a matter of fact, most people go to work for about eight to ten hours and probably only work three to four hours. What do they do with the other time? Waste it. People don't have time-management issues, because you can't stop the clock or call timeouts. If you are finding yourself losing time, most likely you have a priority issue. Focus on what leads you to a sale and nothing more. As a matter of fact, write this saying down on the back of a card or a sheet of paper and read it over and over. "Am I doing the most productive activity that will lead to a sale right now?"

Sales is all about planning, discipline, and accountability. Self-discipline molds, corrects, and improves your performance. It's easy to say, a little tougher to follow through with. I heard that self-discipline is like when the rubber hits the road, or when you put your money where your mouth is. Less talking and more doing usually works with self-discipline. Just do it—don't wait for everything to be right—just do it. I can tell you this, throw effort and commitment into your work and you will be more productive.

You were not put on this earth to be average. Every day is your best day and every day you give your best, and on the days you can only give 50%, then just give 100% of the 50%. That's why I came up with 50–100.

That is, the world's greatest closer's Fifty Tips to Giving 100% Today. How many times have you seen people come to work *not ready to work*? They bring the night with them, don't they? Their problems seem to follow them like a ball and chain. Complaining about everything helps them get through their crisis, and in the meantime, they aren't working or being productive. When in doubt, do yourself a favor—put in effort at work. The results are amazing. Just work it, baby!

How Can I Walk With The Rich?

You can walk with the rich when you finish your work day or before you get to work. Why not have your day planned out the day before, so that when you come to work you are mentally prepared to sell and close? How many times have you gone to work and said, "I was busy all day long, but didn't get a damn thing done!" Quit confusing activity with productivity. Today, write out your plan for the day. It's like programming a GPS in your car—most likely you won't get lost on the way to your destination. It almost seems too easy, doesn't it? Just do it. Take out a sheet of paper and plan your day right now. When you get one activity done, move on to the next one. At some point multitasking has to stop.

Daily Vitamins—Take Your Vitamins to be Prepared

There is a combination of *daily vitamins* that the world's greatest closer takes everyday to maintain a healthy mind and body. Great salespersons have to take care of themselves, as sales is a demanding mental job, and at times can be physically demanding. If you don't take care of yourself, then you may go into a slump. The world is challenging and so is life, and if you aren't charged up or fired up, your prospects will look at you like you are a tired old salesperson. You won't be able to sell if you have that kind of look. Plus, when your energy level goes down, so does the mental part of selling. The results can be fatal to your sale. If you remember the movie *Miracle*, which was about the 1980 Olympic gold hockey team, famed coach Herb Brooks said, "The legs feed the wolf." What he was saying is, you have to be in shape both mentally and physically.

Prospects typically buy three things you, your product, and your company. Taking these *daily vitamins* will help you maintain your energy level throughout the day. The benefit is that you will be able to close more sales. They are:

A—Attitude of gratitude—Be happy that you woke up today, be

thankful for everything you have no matter where you are in life. You have it better than most; not as good as some, but on the whole you are better and improving. An attitude of gratitude will wipe out cynicism and the daily pollutants that the world gives you every day. Look at this way, you don't have to get up, you get to get up, you don't have to go to work, you get to go to work, you don't have to be poor, you just choose to be. Life is about choices and how you get into action to reach your choices. Too many people have hang-UPS, and they can't let them go, or they have hate in their souls. Others won't ever forgive people, so while the offender has gone on, they are still feeling offended. Why not let it go? Why hold a grudge? Why waste your life on things you can't control? To get control, you give up control.

B—Belief in self—If you can believe in yourself and your abilities to close anyone, you are three quarters of the way there. Don't let doubt creep in, don't let the world tell you what you can't do. Throw out some of your old rules that have kept you in a mental prison. You hear it all the time: you aren't as good as they are, you're way too small, you're the new person here, that sale was just luck, you were in the right place at the right time, or that won't happen around here. Keep your faith with you at all times along with your belief that you can do it. If you believe in yourself you are 75% there already.

C—Courage—Courage in French means strength of heart. Courage goes past where fear stops. The world's greatest closer isn't afraid to ask for the order or afraid of rejection. Get used to rejection, it's part of selling, I didn't say you have to love it, but every time you ask for the order you have a 50% chance they will say yes and a 50% chance they will say no. Don't let fear stand in your way. Fear is nothing but a dark room where people develop their negatives. Fear is ignorance and can be destroyed with information and knowledge. You don't get paid for what you know, you get paid for what you do with what you know. When you get in front of your next prospect repeat this over and over—they are not going to say no to me, I am going to convince them to say yes to me—repeat it over and over and then go and close it.

D—Determination—So many times, victory is just around the corner from failure. The world's greatest closers are so determined to be number one that they won't let anything get in their way. All you have to do is go a little faster, a little further, be a little better and you will be far ahead of your competition.. Most selling victories are right around the corner from failure. Determination is making decisions to go forward in spite of fear. So many people that enter into sales, say, well if this doesn't work out, I can always go back. If you say that you will die in your new job. Or you hear people say, "Well I have to keep my options open." You will be doomed to fail.

E—Enthusiasm—The world's greatest closer takes this vitamin every day. Enthusiasm is maintained when you keep your daily goals and long-term goals in front of you. Show me a less-tha–enthusiastic person and I will show you a dead living person who doesn't have their goals in front of them. Keep your goals right in front of you, repeat them out loud daily. Write out at least a few goals a day and watch what happens. Learn more about your product so you can throw enthusiasm at your prospect. You will close more sales just by being enthusiastic. Prospects don't like buying from worn-out, below-average, weak, pathetic, mealy-mouthed salespeople. They like to buy from energetic, positive-thinking people who can transfer their enthusiasm to their prospects.

F—Faith—You can't really see faith, can you? The world's great closers have faith in themselves, their product, and the company they work for. If you follow all the steps throughout the sale, then most likely you will be able to close the sale. No matter how many *no*s you hear, you will soon hear yes. You can't give up, let up, or shut up, until you close them up.

G—Goodness—The more you give to your prospects, the more

they will give to you. Go out of your way to serve your customer first, before you try to sell them. Treat all your prospects with respect and honesty, and they will buy from you. Seventy percent of customers will buy from you, just because they like you. When they like you, they buy from you.

H—Hope—The word hope means Helping Other People Excel. I believe it was Zig Ziglar who said it best: "You can have everything you want in life, if you just help enough other people get what they want."

I—Integrity—Integrity isn't something you take off like a coat. You either have it or you don't. Deceitful salespeople may get away with lying for only so long; the problem is that you have to remember your lies.

J—Juice—means Join Us In Creating Enthusiasm—You can get really powered up if you work together with your team.

K—Knowledge—The average college education has about an eighteen-month shelf life. Keeping an open ear to new ideas and knowledge will keep you up to date and will freshen your mind. Knowledge is the frontier of tomorrow. As long as you have an appetite to improve, you won't ever get enough.

L—Labor—I haven't heard of too many people who passed away from working hard, but I have heard about people passing away from lack of work. When in doubt, throw hard work and effort at doubt—you can't be stopped.

M—Motivation—We should call it motiv–action. It's an inside job. Keep your goals in front of you so that you can stay motivated. If you lose sight of your goals, soon your motivation will go away, too.

N—No Negativity—Go today without saying one negative word or watching the negative news channel. Go one day without criticizing people or making fun of them. Look for all the goods today in life instead of the wrongs in life or the wrongs in people.

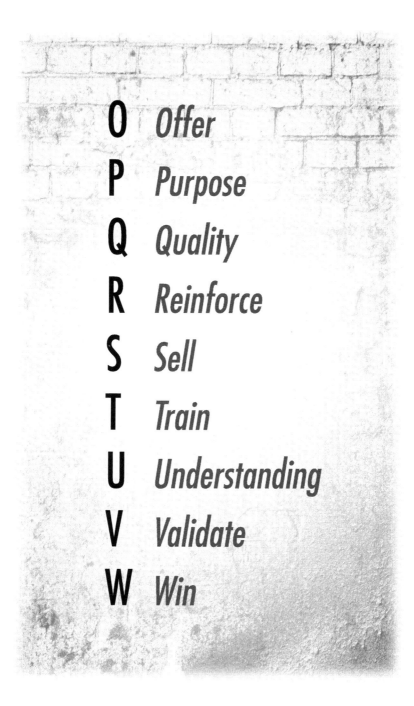

O   *Offer*

P   *Purpose*

Q   *Quality*

R   *Reinforce*

S   *Sell*

T   *Train*

U   *Understanding*

V   *Validate*

W   *Win*

Let's get ready to sell so you can close right now

The definition of the word *sell* is important to everybody, and it doesn't matter what you sell. Understanding the word sell will help you close more sales. Why would you enter a career where you didn't really understand what you are supposed to do?

Sell—I have asked so many salespeople what the word sell means and quite often most salespeople don't know what the word sell means. There are several definitions of the word sell; the most common definition of the word sell is "to convince people of what you are selling." The best way to convince someone to buy your product or services is *first* to get behind what you are selling. If you don't know your product, then you will have a hard time convincing them to buy. When that happens, your prospect will sense it and then make up some sort of objection that you might not be able to overcome.

What does the word *convince* mean? I went to a website "www. answers.com" and typed in the word convince and it said that it means "to persuade someone." Since selling is convincing, and convincing is persuading, then persuading means getting your prospect to take action to buy your product or your services.

Your prospects won't buy from you *if* you lack the skills and confidence in yourself and your services or products. There is an old saying that goes like this: "If you have to think, you stink." If you don't stick to the script, then you slip. Most salespeople will lose sales just because they aren't prepared and haven't found out their customers' buying needs and wants. Through an effective investigation, you will be able to determine your prospects' needs, motivation, and the ability to find a solution to their problem or need. Closing isn't a matter of taking a big breath and saying, "Okay, here comes the close." Closing is a process that begins the first time you meet or talk to a prospect. The closing is just another question that is added to the selling process.

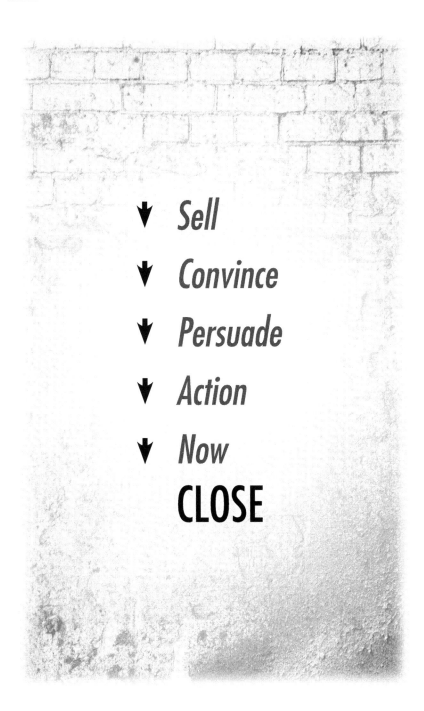

▼ *Sell*

▼ *Convince*

▼ *Persuade*

▼ *Action*

▼ *Now*

CLOSE

The Script

Selling is like a play; there are certain scenes and acts, and most of the time selling is done on a stage. You are an actor if you are selling something. Rehearsing what you have to say will help you with your script. Everything you say is a script, no matter how you look at it. Generally salespeople don't like scripts; however, no matter what you say, it's a script. Where do you find your scripts? Salespeople find them mostly by trial and error, other salespeople, experience, books, classes, and training materials. If you don't agree with me, I understand. However, look at this script.

I love you—it's a script and normally works when you put your voice, body language, and words together. Now look at this script: I hate you—that script won't get you very far with anyone. There are three words, yet only one was different. When selling, your sale is a process. You can't do the ending before the beginning. If you ask for the order too soon, then the nos get bigger. The world is a stage and if you can act right, you will win the award. Look at any actor who wins the Oscar. They read a script and soon become that character. That's not really them up there, in the movie. It's them portraying the character.

Breaking Down the Word Selling

SELL
CONVINCE
PERSUADE
ACTION
NOW
CLOSE

How do I master scripts? — How Do I Climb the Mountain?

The will to improve and practice has to be stronger then the will to sell. Not many salespeople like to practice; it shows their flaws and where they need to improve. When I do my seminars, people are afraid that I am going to call on them to role-play a script. I've actually seen people take their name tags off or turn over their tent name cards. When I walk by them they look away. Why would people be afraid to practice in between customers? Doesn't it make sense to practice and iron out your scripts so that when you are on stage you don't have to wing it? You don't want to be a wing-it guy or girl.

You have to read, write, speak, and record your scripts some thirty times so that when called on, you don't have to think about what you are going to say. The only way to be quick with the mouth is to practice, so that any time a prospect throws an objection at you, you are prepared to handle and overcome it.

1200 seconds or twenty minutes

Developing your skills takes time and devoting twenty minutes—which is 1200 seconds a day—will help you develop your skills and maintain the ones you have. It's literally crazy to warm up on your prospects. Your tongue is in a wet spot and it tends to slip up quite a bit. Think of your vocabulary as your armor and like most things that shine, you have to take time and polish it. Your words are the same, but you have to take out your scripts and polish your words, until they flow naturally.

Proper Practice Prevents Poor Performance

All you have to do is get some three-by-five cards and then write the objections on one side and your responses on the other side. When you start your day, take out your flash cards and practice your scripts and responses. If you are new in sales, it will require you to practice more. Taking fifteen to twenty minutes a day will help you improve your responses, which will improve your confidence and closing ratios. If you are a tenured salesperson, most likely you can just gloss over the flash cards. The best way to reinforce a script is through consistent practice and reinforcement. The world's greatest closer is always prepared to sell and close, and soon you will be, too.

Open your mind up to practicing daily

When learning a new script it literally takes some thirty times of reading the script perfectly, writing it word for word, role playing, and eventually recording it. This is how I learned to become the world's greatest closer. I would write out the script on a three-by-five card and then I would repeat it over and over until it was perfect, word for word. If you start changing the words while practicing, you will be all over the place. Here is a script on overcoming objections, see if you can learn it word perfect:

Isolating Objections — Sixteen words to remember.

Salesperson: "Other than that, is there any other reason why we couldn't wrap it up right now?"

It comes out to sixteen words, close the book and see if you can say it word perfect right now. Most people want to change it by a word or two. When you practice, you practice word for word so that your brain understands that you don't take shortcuts. If you can learn one script perfectly, then it will be easier to learn all the other scripts faster and your closing ratios will improve quickly.

Blow the Lid off your income

L *Learn*

I *Improve*

D *Do*

L *Losing*

A *Attitude*

C *Can*

K *Kill*

But But But…

I knew the buts were coming. I hate change, I hate learning new scripts, it's not me, I have to be me, I don't like learning other people's scripts. Okay, I understand that. Remember, in the beginning, it sounds like a script, but soon it won't sound like a script—it will become you. Actors are given a script and soon they become the character because they have practiced the words, over and over, until they win the Academy Award. Then we see them on the street and they are just normal people. You can do the same thing if you are willing to learn, practice, role play, and act on what you learned. Think of any sport you took up, it's awkward in the beginning, and after repeated practice, you can almost call your shots. Selling is the same way. The will to practice is even more important than the will to win. The game is a reflection of your practice, your paycheck is a direct reflection of your skills.

Why Do I Have to Write It and Record It?

Okay, here is my secret to learning, We all learn different ways, you learn by auditory, visual, and kinetic methods. With scripts, if you write them out they are being seen visually and those pictures are being developed in your subconscious mind and when needed, your conscious mind reaches down to your subconscious mind. When you hear the scripts after recording, your ears open up to hearing it because it's your voice. You've heard it your entire life, so you are more apt to listen to yourself, since you talk to yourself all day long. How many times have you been in a workshop or class, and you miss what the instructor is saying? How many times have you heard people say to you, "I told you about this, how come you didn't do it the way I told you?" We all hear pretty much the same, but how we take in the material is another thing. Think back to when you were a child and your parents told you a million times to clean your room. After hearing them nag at you, you just learned how to tune it out, didn't you?

Why Can't I Get to the Top? The Hike to Success Starts with One Step

You can get to the top of the leader board if you have a burning desire to get there. Whatever you aim for is usually what you hit. Don't settle for average; aim high and you will get there. Believe me there are many more openings at the top than at the bottom. The air is a lot cleaner at the top than at the bottom. Give your best and the best will come to you. Life is so easy, what you throw out is what you get back. Give a little, get a little, throw out a lot, and a tidal wave of good will come back to you.

Most salespeople's problem is that they start at the bottom of sales, then they look up and see the ladder in front of them. In this frenetic world that has turned into a one-click download generation, they want

to start at the top of the ladder or take one big leap and miss most of the rungs and land near the top. Good luck to you. Sometimes you can leap a couple of rungs. For the most part you have to take it step by step. This old wise saying still stands true today: "Inch by inch it's a cinch, but by the yard it's too hard." Are you starting to see what the world's greatest closer is doing to you? You are being sold to do better than you were and to get into action, which will bring you to your goals faster than your talk!

CHAPTER FOUR

Why Salespeople Fail

Sales Manager: "Hey, Andy Average, how come you haven't had a good year this year?"

Andy Average: "Well, it's been a weird year, I can tell you that. January is horrible because it is right after the holidays, and February is a short month. March is useless because everybody is getting ready for tax season. April is all about the tax refund or they have to pay taxes. May is crazy—everybody is getting married or getting ready for summer vacation, and June sucks, all the kids are getting out of school and going on vacation. July is brutal, everyone is on vacation, and August isn't any better, all the families and kids are coming back from vacation. Soon September is here, now all the moms are getting the kids ready for back to school, October is all about the change of seasons, plus trick or treat is coming. As for November, Thanksgiving is coming, and last here comes December—everybody is at the mall shopping.

Sales Manager: Good job, Andy, you have more excuses then any one person I have ever met. I'm going to help you out, okay? Andy, you can work, you just can't work here! You're fired.

Just Over Broke:
A JOB is what you work at a CAREER is what you develop

C — CHOICES
A — ATTITUDE
R — ROLE–PLAY–REINFORCE
E — ENTHUSIASM
E — EFFORT
R — RESULTS

It doesn't matter what profession you are in or what type of job you work at. The world's great closers look for opportunity no matter what profession they are in or what type of job they have. I know a lot of people who have turned a job into a career. The word job spelled out is Just Over Broke. If you aren't in the mode of improving, then you are in the mode of dying, If you are in the mode of surviving, you will always be a *just-enough-to-get-by person*. Career-minded people are always in the mode of developing their skills and their habits over their lifetime. You must have a thirst to improve yourself and it has to be a daily activity. Since you have to shower everyday then why don't you take time to improve yourself every day; they go hand in hand.

Remember that Zig Ziglar said, "We all need a checkup from the neck up."

Remember the movie *A Few Good Men*, with Tom Cruise and Jack Nicholson? In the court scene, Tom yelled at Jack, "I need the truth!" Jack came back and said, "You can't handle the truth!"

Most salespeople can't handle the truth themselves. If you ask them why they don't work for X Company anymore, most salespeople would soften their answer with, "It was weird, management wouldn't work with me," or "I wasn't their favorite," or "it was really hard for me," or "I just wasn't for sales."

The Truth Will Set you Free!

Why don't you just tell the truth: You failed. You got blown out for low production. Why? Because your heart, mind, and soul were not in sync. If you master your craft, then you craft your sales.

Why do salespeople lose sales? Why do they fail?

They fail because they don't have enough tools in their toolbox to close the sale. They keep making the same mistakes over and over. The cost of losing a sale is gigantic at times, isn't it? Nobody likes to lose. Salespeople fail for many different reasons. For the most part it's because they don't have the right words to say at the right time. Combine that with a "lack attitude" (lack means Losing Attitudes Can Kill) and you will start to see a pattern. Can you afford to keep making the same mistakes? I often think about how many salespeople quit selling because they couldn't overcome objections or rid themselves of their mistakes.

Twelve Easy Sales Mistakes That Salespeople Make Daily

1. **The lack attitude**—A person with a lack attitude has lost their passion, the ability to persuade, the confidence to ask for the order, and the skills to handle the objection. Get over it and get ready for the next call or prospect. Get focused and let go of your negative experiences. A weak mind will dwell on failures all day long, and soon you won't even have the guts to ask for the order. If you quit visiting your negative attitude, soon it will

leave you and you will be positive. Don't pay attention to negativity, and it won't pay attention to you.

2. **A whiner's attitude instead of a winners attitude.** There are
too many salespeople who use excuses—a crutch to hold them
up when sales are down. It gets to the point where these people
are professional excusiologists. The more excuses you use the
more power you will have to use to defend them. It's time to
get off the complain train and get on the win train. I can hear
the therapist now. So what is your problem? I need help, I'm so
weak that I can't close sales right now. Do you think any of it is
your fault? No, I know for sure. Why is that? Have you done
anything to improve yourself? No, I don't have time, plus that
self-help stuff doesn't work anyway, I tried it once and I felt like
a goof. Okay, have you thought about maybe working on your
skills? No, I tried it once and it didn't work. I understand.

3. **Not enough skills.** If you want to be the world's greatest closer,
then you need to go back to the school of selling. Education
is priceless. Learn more, then you sell more. People who fail
usually fail due to lack of professional selling skills. If you aren't
growing, then you are dying.

4. **Experience.** I had to throw this one in. There are so many salespeople who have been in selling for years but can't get to the top.
Yet when you talk to them, they say, "I have forgotten more then
you will ever know." True, you have forgotten more, because you
aren't taking time to hit the refresh button called training. You
hear these veteran salespeople say, "You have to be in this business
for years before you become successful." Oh really? Then how
come a salesperson has been in their business for ten years is still
only an average salesperson? It's because they quit learning how
to sell years ago. My question is this: Do they have ten years of
selling experience or the first year repeated ten times?

5. **Shortcuts:** If shortcuts were the way to sell, then we wouldn't have a normal process to follow. Shortcuts are pay cuts. When you take shortcuts in the selling process, your prospect will soon smell your commission breath. If you can't find the time to do it right the first time, then will you find time to do it right the next time?

6. **Not prepared to sell today:** What if your airline pilot showed up today looking like yesterday was still with him? What if he showed up and said, "I think on this flight we will wing it?" If you wing your sales, you will soon be flying around looking for a new job.

7. **Poor follow-up:** Follow-up is the key to selling more then what you sell right now. Most salespeople give up then follow up, they treat follow-up like it's a life sentence without parole. Did you know that most salespeople quit following up after the first follow-up call. Yes, it's true; they can't handle rejection so they quit following up and that's when your competition moves in and steals their business. The weak-minded salesperson considers follow-up as punishment.. The prospects that are easier to buy from, are your previous prospects. Get back on the phone, start a email, text message or belly to belly campaign and go to work. If you don't plant the seeds, or mind your crop, it will soon be a field of weeds.

8. **Bad habits:** This right here will lead you to the door called failure. So many salespeople have developed bad habits over their careers and are manipulated by them. Self discipline is the arch enemy of bad habits. Good habits will lead you to becoming the world's greatest closer. Change is hard, change is constant, when replacing a bad habit, remember the law of the forest will tell you, you have to replace the bad habit with a new

habit. If not, the old habit, which is your master, will come back and you will be a slave to it forever.

9. **Activity management/time management:** They spend more time majoring in non-productive selling activities and usually you see them cram their entire selling month in the last week of the month.

10. **Looking for another job while they are still at their current job:** They are quitters, and soon they only give a little effort and before you know it, they are gone.

11. **They can't get off the complain train:** As crazy as it sounds, people like to complain to others about nothing. They whine and whine until they either feel better about their whine or until they can sell people a case of whine.

12. **Worn-out sales presentation:** Nothing worse than listening to some tired, worn-out, below-average, mealy-mouthed, weak, lazy salesperson's presentation. I watched a presentation by a sports figure not too long ago. His story was amazing, yet his presentation was weak, rushed, tired, worn-out, and you could tell that he has said it so many times that they were both worn out. The energy was gone, along with his passion to tell it. What a shame! He cheated his audience, but I bet you he picked up the full speaking fee. You might as well just mail it in. Start hitting the refresh button. Energize yourself along with your presentation.

George's fifty reasons why salespeople fail

- I watch negative news.
- Nobody likes me.
- I never get a house deal or anything like that.
- I don't like where I live.
- I hate my job.

- Management won't work with me.
- My life sucks.
- I'm broke.
- I read the misery news everyday.
- My personal problems weigh me down.
- It's never a good time to sell.
- Our product isn't as good as our competitor's product.
- This is only a temporary job for me.
- I'm going to retire soon, so why work hard?
- That FNG makes me sick.
- They don't pay me enough to do that kind of work.
- I only do what I get paid for.
- I'm not the owner's son or daughter.
- The economy sucks.
- It's always raining here.
- The world is messed up.
- I don't even know if I will be here tomorrow.
- Why work hard? I'm still broke.
- I hate change but wish I had more change in my pocket.
- I can't get over it when my prospect says no to me.
- Rejection ruins my day.
- We already gave that a try; it didn't work.
- We don't have the resources.
- I think it will get better soon, I hope.
- I'm too old for this job.
- I wish I was better looking.
- That won't ever happen to me.
- I'm still blaming my parents.
- I grew up deprived.
- Someday.
- Selling is tough today; it's not like the old days.

- That's the way the ball bounces I guess.
- Nobody told me.
- Corporate is out of their mind.
- What's the use; nobody listens to me anyway.
- The seasons control my selling income.
- I'm a professional excusiologist.
- Why me?
- *If only...* If only I had more skills. If only I were younger. If only the pay were better. If only I were here longer. If only If only If only If only if only, If only I worked smarter!
- Bad apples will only spoil the bunch, plus I hate apples anyway.
- Uses weak words such as I might, I think, I can't, I'll try.
- House mouse—salespeople expect management to always spoon feed them sales.
- Who cares?

Can you now see why the above will never rise to be the greatest closer in the world? No wonder they can't win. The results of your efforts and beliefs will be measured by your paycheck and income. There has to be a point where you aren't using the blame game or the blame train to control your income. How often I have heard people say, "Oh it's the market, nobody is buying, the weather is horrible, last year we did a lot better." First off, if you want to hear about last year, watch the History Channel, same thing with the Weather Channel. Don't get caught up listening to that less-than-meaningful information. If you want to sell more, it's up to you, if you want to use the seasons of the year as excuses, then read on.

"It's impossible to be perfect, but there's nothing wrong with being honest." —Rick Warren Purpose Driven Life

CHAPTER FIVE

What Can Be Done About It?

There are far too many salespeople who are good at a little of this and a little of that and never really accomplish their daily plan. Andrew Carnegie of US Steel had a production expert come in. Carnegie wanted to know how to make his company more productive. The expert started telling Mr. Carnegie about how management needs to be trained more and so on. Carnegie stopped him in his conversation and said, "Look, we don't need to learn more, what we need to learn is how to be more productive! I will pay you a lot of money if you can show me that." The expert said, "Take out a sheet of paper and write five activities that you need to accomplish. When you get done with one, cross it off and move on to number two." The results were incredible. At times it's better to keep things simple.

Life is simple if you use my KISS system.

K — KEEP
I — IT
S — SIMPLE
S — SALESPERSON OR SALES MANAGER

TIPS = To Insure Performance Salesperson

People Make Mistakes — Mistakes Don't Make People

Quitters will never win. You can't be afraid to take chances or make mistakes. For years I have said that risk taking is job security. Will you fail at times? Yes. Will you make mistakes? Yes. Will you take shortcuts at time? Yes. Can you turn your setbacks into comebacks? *YES.* You can work yourself through your mistakes by understanding where you made your mistakes and then being honest with yourself. There are times when the truth hurts, but the faster you run to the truth, the faster you leap up the rungs on the ladder. The world's greatest closers aren't afraid to look in the mirror. Any time you use excuses you will need alibis or lies. Successful closers don't need explanations for success. If you look at their report card, which is their paycheck, you will normally find straight As or more zeros at the end of their income.

The definition of a failure is a person who gives up, lets up, shuts up, and ends up quitting and looking for something easier to do. If at first you don't succeed, try, try, try again! Closers don't use that saying, because it would be ridiculous to do the same thing over and over expecting a different result. That is the definition of insanity, according to Einstein. If at first you don't succeed, find out why, then adapt, adjust, and attack! It will be tough to be perfect, but it's easier to be honest with yourself. Sometimes being honest is like taking medicine, you hate the bitter taste, but long after the taste is gone, you enjoy the rewards of the medicine. The truth has the same effect.

Start Doing Instead of Talking — George's Justs

Action will bring you to your goals faster than anything else. Start working more and talking less. You will sell more.

Just work, just take action, just get in the car and get going, just get in front of more prospects, just pick up the phone, just send out more emails, just get out of the office and be more productive, just get out and network more, just learn more how to sell, just practice a bit more, just learn more about your product, just follow up more, just be more organized, just use more of your selling time to sell, just ask more prospects for the sale, just learn how to get over rejection, just come to work to actually work, just ask for more referrals, just take better care of yourself, just make one more stop for the day, just make one more phone call for the day, just work a bit harder than others, just be nicer to people, just serve people before you try to sell them, just have an attitude of gratitude, just do it!

I remember a movie where a character said that his boss was like pig vomit. I have worked with such a person. I will never mention their name but I can tell you that this person was a manager ahead of me while I was in sales. The person was disgusting, crude, rude, and was the worst person I ever worked with. You have a few choices when you face this. You can quit and move on to another business, you can become one of those persons, or you can just learn how to get along with the situation and work with what you have and not allow the person to offend you anymore. The offender moves on, but many people hold a grudge. I've never seen a perfect work place. What you need to learn is how to get along with what you don't like about people. Do that and you can get along. I just don't see why you would allow someone to bother you and let them affect your sales. Forget about it. Move on and control what you can and what you can control are right here:

Nobody can be perfect but you can be honest with yourself. You can control a few things when it comes to selling and if you can get hold of these three it will help you stay focused and not get caught up in the backdraft of work. I was at a client's business and while consulting there, the sales team told me about some of the problems at their place of work. Finger-pointing should be outlawed. Not once did the salespeople turn and point at themselves. Some of the employees wanted to quit or had given up while working there. Look, there are only so many things that you can control and the best way to get control is to give up control. If you can't change it, then let it go and get back to what you do best—selling. Do you like losing money? Well if you get caught in these traps, it will strangle your income and soon your job. Every job, business, or career has problems. Learn how to get around, through, or along with the problem. These are the three things you can control:

1. Attitude
2. Activities
3. Energy

Learning how to change and control your attitude will help you in your journey as a salesperson. Focusing and managing your activi-

ties will drive you to your goal. I have heard over and over that an accurate mind, with accurate activities, will accurately bring you to your goals.

There is nothing worse than a salesperson who is running on empty and can't focus or get excited to sell and close. Energy drinks are okay for a while, but soon they lose their effectiveness. A balanced diet is key to maintaining your energy throughout the day. Just look at how many times you hear salespeople say, "I'm so done, I'm burned out, I'm so out of here." Then you look at their watch and it's only three p.m.. You have one body, so why not treat it right and respect it? Fast food is called fat food for a reason. It's not always the healthiest of choices. It seems like when people are tired and hungry they eat more than they can handle. How often have you eaten too much at lunch and then said, "I'm done for the day, I'm toast." Eat right to sell right.

World's Greatest Closer Habits and Traits

Do you want to be the world's greatest closer or a loser? Are you willing to work for it or are you a lottery player who plays the easy way to get rich—spend a buck, make a million? The weak don't want to pay the price for success. I call them lottery salespeople. You can spot them a mile away. They give a bit but expect a lot. That thinking will never bring you to the top of your game. As for *luck*, you have it but you just have to use it. Check out what the word *luck* means:

L—LABOR
U—UNDER
C—CORRECT OR CONTROLLED
K—KNOWLEDGE

Luck is met at the intersection where preparation meets opportunity. You aren't lucky, you are good.

—Elmer Letterman: worldofquotes.com

CHAPTER SIX

The Basics — Be a Salesperson in Control

. . . .

"Commission possible—not mission impossible!"

The Basics of Selling and Closing — Be A Salesperson In Control

When you are selling at work or you are out selling at appointments, there must be a path that you follow to close more sales. No matter where you work or who you work for, you will always hear management say, "Get back to basics." In any type of sales, there has to be a foundation from which you need to build your sale. The basics are just about the same for any profession where selling takes place. You can always take shortcuts, but don't forget shortcuts are pay cuts. There will always be exceptions to the rules of selling. I know you have probably have closed customers without following the steps to the sale. We all have done that; however, don't make the exception the norm. When in doubt ,go back to the basics. I can tell you this: You will leave them, but they will never leave you. They really don't change. It's the product or the technology that changes.

I have outlined a basic selling timeline for most sales professionals. You can use this selling process no matter what you sell. The benefits to following the basics will be profitable to you. I have been a sales manager over the course of my years and every time I see salespeople miss steps to the sale, it costs them money. Look at the word basic and what it spells.

B — Be
A — A
S — Salesperson
I — In
C — Control

The steps of the basics can help you close more sales right now!

STEP 1: DRESS WELL AND BEHAVE NICELY.

I can't tell you how many salespeople miss sales because of the way they dress or act. The first impression is important to your success. I have heard many salespeople say, "They can take it or leave it." Don't worry, they will leave it. There are so many different sales professions and you have to dress accordingly, no doubt about it. If your career demands a business suit, then wear it. If your job standards are casual dress, dress casually. For some dumb reason, casual dress became the norm years ago. Prospects said that a business suit was intimidating. If that is true, then why didn't most salespeople's income go up to with the switch to casual dress?

While I was consulting at a multimillion dollar sales business, the sales manager was trying to sell me on the relaxed look. I just couldn't and wouldn't buy it. Dress according to your type of business. It reminds me of the time I went ski-boat shopping and I took my young family with me. We were in the showroom and were greeted by a salesperson who was wearing a blue polo shirt buttoned up, shorts, and deck shoes. He just looked like a boat salesperson. A tie and suit would have been too much for this type of sale. We bought, but we didn't buy until he went through the selling basics. He was a master salesperson who knew his product, backed with his enthusiasm that what he was selling was the best boat out there. His rapport and questioning were incredible. My children and I picked out where they were going to sit. Here we were in a warehouse, and I thought I was on the water already.

Prospects need to have mental ownership before they have financial ownership. The salesperson went for the close and said, "Let me go get some figures for you," and off he went. It got really silent for a minute or two and my son, who was fourteen, said, "Dad, are we going to take it home?" I looked at him and said, "Well, son, we don't want to rush into things. We should go home and think about it." My son looked up at me and said this; "Dad, I understand, but you do like the boat, don't you?" I said yes. He said, "Dad, is it the boat or the price of the boat that you need to think about?" I told him it was the price. He said, "Dad, take out your checkbook. Let's get this boat and get all this shopping behind us." He then stuck out his hand for me to shake it. He closed his first deal. True story.

If you sell New Age clothing and work in the mall at a clothing store where tattoos and piercings are the norm, then go with it. Just dress accordingly. I really don't care what, just make sure it's clean, pressed, and topnotch for your profession. Don't worry about being overdressed, because you can always dress down, but you once you are dressed down, you can't really come up.

The key is to make the first impression *last*:

L — Looking, Live, Love, Look
A — Acting, always, always, and
S — Sounding, sounding, sounds, sound
T — Think, Talk, thankful, terrific, terrific

Your prospects like to buy from someone who is knowledgeable and makes a great first impression. I recently went to buy a camera and walked into a giant electronics store. I walked around and for the most part was greeted okay. When I found what I was looking for, I summoned a salesperson over to help me. I should have asked him if they sold irons, because he needed one. I just don't get it. If you want to look like somebody who slept in their work clothes, stay home. That is where you belong. I gave him the once-over appraisal, and he wasn't in top market form. When I asked about the camera, his first word was "Umm." I said, "Good comeback." The company is shutting down over a hundred stores.

How Can I Improve My First Impression?

Don't wear your home clothes to work. Make sure you treat your work outfits like a uniform. Common sense applies here. Look in the mirror. Is this the best you can look today? Check your shoes. You can't shine them with a brick or a brillo pad. Don't overdo it with the perfume or cologne. When you walk away, your cologne or perfume should follow you. Wear today's clothing. Retro clothing comes back once in a while. Look for trends and stay within those and you should be okay. As for smoking, cussing, and all that other rude and crude stuff—leave it alone. Your job is to stay above it, not with it. Pros stay above that kind of stuff. It comes down to common sense that just isn't that common. Keep it professional.

STEP 2: Greet your customers and remember their name.

There is nothing worse than forgetting your prospect's name or not greeting them properly. The world's greatest closers don't forget prospect's names, plus they have a standard greeting that works every time.

WGC: "Hi, my name is George. And you are?"

Prospect: "Sam."

WGC: "Sam, thanks for seeing me. It is a great day out, isn't it?

WGC: "Sam, I want to thank you for taking time to see me today."

The key is to repeat your prospects name at the beginning of your first few sentences. There is nothing worse for killing a sale then saying, "I'm sorry, what is your name again?"

STEP 3: Build rapport — No like = no sale.

Slow your prospect down by asking open-ended questions:
Who? What? Where? When? Why? How? Which?
If you don't get your prospect to open up to you, then they will never trust you. People want to buy from friends or people they like and trust. The Internet has really destroyed personal communication. The click of the mouse seems to be more powerful then the word of mouth. I believe that.

STEP 4: Investigate to determine your prospect's wants, needs, motivation, and current problems.

Ask Your Prospect. whats changed in your needs, what has you thinking about purchasing or considering our new product, what cant you live without and what do you really need? THERE'S NOTHING ELSE GOING HERE?

Step 5: FAB — How to do a great job presenting your product and services

The world's greatest closer presents what the customer wants to hear, not what the salesperson wants to talk about. The needs, wants, and motivations should have been discovered during the investigation process. If you have missed that step, then most likely your presentation will be a verbal vomit session where all you do is spit up all over your prospect.

When you are presenting your product, do your best to not use the word *thing*. Thing was something on the old TV show, *The Addams Family*. You don't sell things, you present features, advantages, and benefits.

FAB is not a detergent: **F**eature—what it is, **A**dvantage—what it does, **B**enefit—why they care.

Here is what it means to you:

Feature—what it is, Plasma TV, ABS brakes, cell phone, computer. Features are all over the place in business and everything is a feature. What you don't want to do in your presentation is just talk about the features, because soon it will sound like whatever you are selling is very expensive.

Advantage—What it does, Plasma TV, clearer picture; ABS brakes, helps you stop quicker and gain control; cell phone, Internet options, ease of text or email; Computer, memory, RAM, ease of operation, and so on.

Benefit—why the prospect cares. It is far better to sell benefits, because that is what prospects buy. It's sort of like WIIFM (What's In It For Me). Benefits make customers' lives a lot better. It helps them solve their problems, and in the end, it's a solution.

Example: "Mr. Prospect, you said that safety was important to you. One of the best features about our vehicle is that it has ABS brakes. When you have to apply your brakes suddenly, the brakes pulsate, which will prevent you from skidding and allows you to have control, and the benefit is that you and your family will be safer. Mr. Prospect, you did say that safety was important to you, didn't you?"

Notice how I used the FAB words in the above paragraph, plus I ended my conversation with a yes question, or a trial close.

You can cut and paste the above feature I used and fit what you sell into the above paragraph. If you do that, you will be assured of closing more deals. Remember when you are presenting, you are on a stage which means you are an actor. Don't attempt to do roles you can't fit into. Be natural with your scripts and practice your presentation so that you won't run into as many objections that King Kong couldn't overcome.

Once you get past the rapport and investigation process, now you have to have your game on completely. Most sales are lost right here, though. There are many reasons such as:

1. The salesperson doesn't know their product or services well enough to get behind them with passion.
2. The salesperson didn't determine their prospect's wants, needs, motivation, or clarify exactly what the current product isn't doing for them.
3. The salesperson vomits all over their prospects. If you talk too much, then most likely you will talk yourself right out of the sale.

4. Improper presentation—The salesperson didn't prepare for the presentation.

5. Technology failure—The salesperson didn't check equipment or doesn't know how to use their own equipment.

6. I can tell you this: if you don't know your product well enough to get your prospect into the buying mode, then you can only use price or discounts to close your sale. Most customers and prospects will look at you like you're a bumbling fool if you don't know your product. How can you convince someone else, if you aren't convinced of the product or services? How many times can you keep saying, "I'm new, please excuse my stupidity." Using the *I'm new* card is foolish today since most prospects can research your product or service on the Internet.

Learn your product and services so that you can sell with your heart and passion. To become the world's greatest closer, you have to be able to convince your prospect with your heart, pride, and faith, that if they don't purchase your product they are making a huge mistake and it will cost them dearly. You almost have to be at the point that if they don't buy, you will have to enter therapy to get over the rejection of you and what you sell. It's almost like life or death.

So what is the definition of selling again? Convince, Persuade, Action, Now.

If you don't know your product, then how will you convince your prospect?

Presentation Tips: Don't tell your way through the sale. Selling isn't telling and it's not gushing about your product, program, or services. In fact most salespeople try to say too much about too much. Once you have determined what your prospect's motivation and needs are, the key is to give a FAB presentation.

The features are what you sell, the advantages are what the features do, and the benefits are why your customer cares. Too often salespeople vomit features all over their conversation and when that happens, the price goes up in the prospect's mind. You can lose your sale right there. When selling, the world's greatest closers talk about the features that their prospects care about or need. They then transition to explaining the advantages of what they are selling and then show their prospects the benefits of the features and advantages.

Remember: The feature is what it is—ABS brakes. The advantage is what it does—prevents skidding. The benefit is why they care—safety and peace of mind.

World's Greatest Closer Tip

I would recommend that you write out at least fifty FABS of the product you sell and practice them until they become a natural way of talking and presenting. If you do this, I can assure you that you will be able to *build more sales* that will lead to a bigger paycheck and more job satisfaction. It will reduce objections and help you handle the ones that you do encounter.

BUILD

B — Brief presentation of customers wants, needs, and motivation

U — Uninterrupted — do your best to limit any distractions, cell phones, etc.

I — Interactive — use questions to engage your prospect and keep them interested

L — Listen — Don't talk too much, the ratio should be about 30–40% talking, 60–70% percent listening

D — Develop some urgency to close or do business with you.

STEP 6: Presenting Products and/or Services

Perform an above presentation of your product—Like an academy award presentation. This is why practice is the mother of success.

STEP 7: SELL SERVICE ALONG THE WAY.

Too many times salespeople over-promise and under-deliver. Most prospects want to buy from you, and will if you also sell them on the ease of doing business with you and what they can depend on if their product has a problem. One of the most important steps to the sale is what kind of service you will provide after your prospect has parted with their money and bought your product. It's often one of the biggest concerns of your prospect.

I can remember buying a new vehicle, and I had so many problems with it that I got to know my service advisor on a first-name basis and felt like I knew his family, too. It wasn't his fault that the vehicle broke; what he could control was how he took care of me and my problems. His reaction to my problems was professional and caring. Sell the benefits of why people should do business with you:

- Ease of getting hold of someone
- Service reacts fast
- Service manager's name
- Dependable
- Loaners
- Labor rates
- How long you and the company have been in business

It's one thing for a prospect to buy your product. That doesn't take much time. However, your prospect will own your product more than the time they spend buying it. So service is a big issue. Sell service along the way.

STEP 8 – SECOND-PARTY TESTIMONIALS OR PROOF OF WHY.

Have you ever watched infomercials on TV? They are quite interesting, ranging from home wares, clothing, personal services, body makeovers, etc. Do you really believe what the salesperson says? Or the people who have already purchased the goods?

I watch them when I go out on the road speaking. I'm fascinated not so much by the product, but what the people say about the product. Why is that? They seem real, not actors who are paid to say, "This widget is the best product I have ever seen." People want to know that real people have tried and used your product or services. It gives them a sense of relief and builds their trust in what you are selling; plus, people want to be the same as others. Ask your neighbors. It's like going out to eat. You ask your friends about a restaurant, and if it's good, they will say, you must go to this place, the food was awesome and so was the service.

You will go with enthusiasm, won't you? Do they own the restaurant? No, so why would they brag about it? It was great, and people like to share their successes. If you can back up your selling with a second-party testimonial—letters, photos, or videos, do so. The rewards are great and you will increase your closing ratios almost overnight.

The swimming pool story

Years ago our family bought a new home. We wanted to put a pool in, with a patio and so on. I called a pool company and the salesperson showed up, dressed like a pool construction person, not as a salesperson. We shook hands, he introduced himself to me and asked what kind of pool I wanted. I told him and within a nanosecond he said, oh that would cost $50,000. I just about threw him out of the yard—$50,000, the guy must be nuts.

Well, I travel a lot and soon I got a call from my wife and she told me that another pool person had come by. She told me he was a nice guy, and the kids liked him. He liked hockey which, is what we liked. He was to come back with some drawings and show us what his company could do. I was there for that meeting. He showed up on time, dressed appropriately. We sat at the kitchen table, and he showed us the drawings. I asked him how much the pool would cost, and he bypassed the price twice. We got to the end of his presentation and right before he brought out the contract or agreement, he said, "Oh, here is my proof book of the pools we have installed." He had the photos nicely lined up with letters from his customers. I looked at them and said, "Well you guys do great work, no doubt there." I read the letters; the people loved their pools and the company. I think you know where I am going. Yes, it cost more than $50,000, and I paid for it, but I did get him to throw in a few more palm trees and a barbeque cover.

CHAPTER SEVEN

The Sales Process — The Way to Success

If it's up to me, then it will be

You can hear average salespeople always saying, "That's all they pay around here." No, not really, that's all you're worth. Remember, your skills pay the bills. Don't blame your company or your firm. There are always buyers for your product. If your market is down, then look at it as an opportunity to sell even more. The weak will die and the strong will survive. The only person who controls your paycheck is the one you see in the mirror every day. The power of thought, feeling, and action was discovered by Dr. William James. Everybody has thoughts, which brings on certain feelings, which brings on action. In sales the biggest sell job is to yourself—every day. I sold myself on writing this book and getting to the shelves of the biggest bookstores. I actually would go to the bookstores and walk down the rows of books until I got to sales and management and I took pictures with my camera. I visualized my book being on the shelf. I would then grab it with my mental pictures. I would look at it, look up, and repeat, "My book will be on the shelves, my book will help salespeople become the world's greatest closers." I also said, "I remember the days, the moods, the feelings of what it took to get this done." I was so motivated that nothing could stop me. I told every person I met I was writing this book.

I stopped and started this book so many times. I would get halfway done, and then I would start all over. I wrote on planes, while I was getting a root canal, late at night, early mornings, in the car, at the beach, on vacations, you name a place, I was writing it there. I asked hundreds of people to get involved with me financially to make this happen I heard more nos then yeses and finally one night I was up late and I emailed the man who would back me. I can't thank him enough. His name is Gary Fennelli. I emailed him over and over, I met with him for dinner, I talked to him about this for years, and I asked him again to get involved. I wouldn't take no for answer. I will forever be in debt to him, and the lovely woman of my life, Cyndie. Both of them encouraged me to get this done, I wouldn't be here today without them. I am the world's luckiest man.

It got so bad, that my family and friends weren't friends with me anymore. (LOL) The world's greatest closer is the most persistent person. You can't give up, let up, or shut-up, until you wrap it up!

. . . .

"Keep Asking Until You Hear the Word Yes"

What does your customer expect from today's salesperson?

Being one of the world's great closers can happen for you. I can tell you this, how you treat your prospects will be more important than the product you actually sell. People like to be treated with respect and will

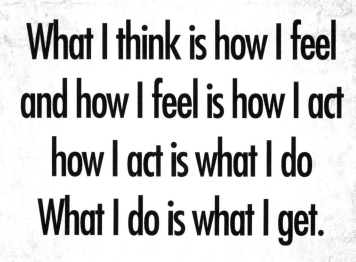

What I think is how I feel and how I feel is how I act how I act is what I do What I do is what I get.

actually tell you what they want and how to be sold. Give or take, some 70+% of prospects will buy from you just because they like you. If they don't like you, then your prospect will come up with reasons why they won't buy, and no matter what you try to do to overcome their reasons, your prospect's objections grow by the second.

Nobody wants to be pressured by some below-average, weak, mealy-mouthed salesperson who doesn't have selling or people skills. Customers are looking for a professional who can show them solutions to fit their needs at a price they can afford, and great service after the sale.

The Three Types of Feeling a Customer Feels When They Don't Know You

Trust   Tension   Belief

Now, you don't have that long to turn those feelings around. It has to be done quickly because your prospect will find a way to get rid of you. It is the same in person or on the phone. Prospects like to deal with people they trust and believe in. If not, the tension rises and the trust factor goes way down. Turning around the above feelings can happen if you look like a professional, and get people on common ground with you. When prospects talk about-themselves, they no longer are thinking about you. They have to be won over at the beginning of the sales process. That is called the buying process. They buy you, then you sell, and then you can close them. Under normal circumstances people come to you for one reason—to buy, if you go to them, then sometimes you have to create an atmosphere for them to buy. Selling is an art that takes time to master. The best way to sell your customer is by getting them on common ground and getting them to open up to you. Do that and the close is easier.

What do customers expect today?

1. *Honesty and integrity*: somebody who makes great eye contact when they speak and doesn't have to use lies to sell. When you lie, you have to remember what you lied about. If you promise, then deliver on the promise. Honesty and integrity are something you have or don't have. I was with a high-powered client, an owner of a company, and we were talking about another product and service that he used. What this salesperson sold him was worth about $750,000 a year. This client told me how he wanted to get rid of the salesperson and the product. I asked him why? He told me the salesperson was not honest with him. He just wanted to hear the truth, whether or not he should focus his efforts and money in a certain way to market his company. The client told me, why can't the salesperson be honest with me? I asked him, if he was honest with you, would you keep his services? He said yes. What an expensive loss of commission that's going to be.

2. *Wow factor*: Give your prospect more then they expect, whether they buy or not. Go the extra mile or two, do the activities that below-average salespeople won't do. Remember that every time you go the extra mile, your prospects will feel more obligated to you. Nothing wrong with sending out a small thank-you card for the visit, text, email, or letter. Do this, thank them not for buying from you but somehow you look forward to the day, you can serve them. I remember when I was going for a job interview. I didn't get the job, however within three days, I sent a thanks-for-not-hiring-me letter to the CEO. It blew him away. I eventually got the job, it was then worth $ 200,000 a year. They never forgot the letter, he told me it was the first one they had ever received. I don't have the original letter but it went something like this:

Dear Sirs:

I wanted to thank you for your time and effort today, I also wanted to thank you for rejecting and not hiring me. I can see the changes I need to improve on so that one day you will say yes to hiring me.

I went on to learning everything I possibly could to getting hired by the company, it took me several interviews, recording videos of their training, sending them in, making over 100 phone calls, and being rejected a couple of more times. I can remember practicing their scripts for hours and hours, no matter where I was, no matter how late it was, no matter what I was doing, I was going to practice until I got the job. I got it, while there were over 450 applicants for the job, I finally won it out. Eventually I became the employee of the year while receiving the Rolex for my hard work, commitment and dedication. You can do the same thing, you can ask for whatever you want in life, but at some point, you have to pay the price for success, it's called work my friends. it's often missed by most because it's dressed up in overall's and it's dirty. That was Napoleon Hill talking there, author of Think And Grow Rich.

3. *Follow up:* Follow up with your sold and unsold prospects. Just don't sell them and expect them to follow up with you. Your follow-up has to be consistent and ongoing. Roughly only about 10% of salespeople follow up. If you followed up you really wouldn't have any competition. You have to quit thinking that follow-up is punishment. By default if you follow up, then your sale will be smoother sailing along with a higher closing ratio.

4. *Remember their name:* This is important to stay connected with them. Your prospect has heard their name their entire life. It shows that you care when you remember their name and use it. When you meet your prospect, repeat their name right away at least four to five times, use their name at the beginning of each sentence.

5. *Get them smiling*: If you can get your prospect to warm up, you can get them to smile and laugh. Keep it light, keep if fun, and keep it professional.

6. *Negotiate like a professional salesperson*: Nobody wants to deal with an amateur when they are buying. Don't use ineffective closes such as, "What would it take to earn your business," or offer to drop the price.

7. *Sell solutions, not products:* And watch your income rise. Prospects who are in the market to purchase something have a void. Sell the solution and the sale will be a lot easier to close. Find out why they are looking for your services or products. Most of the time a situation has come up or something has to be replaced or improved. The key is to find your buyer's motivation and what has changed that has them looking for something new. The best way to determine what your prospect's needs and wants is by asking questions. If you ask your way through the sale, you will probably close your sale; if you tell your way, you will lose your sale. Today's customer is looking for an interactive salesperson. Don't believe me—look at how interactive web technology is today.

8. *Get your customer on common ground:* Find out their likes, where they go, places they visit, sports they enjoy. Talk people, then products. You will be the world's greatest closer if you become more interested in your prospects than in being more interesting.

"People don't care how much you know until they know how much you care." Simple but effective. Prospects will open up if you give them a chance to open up, build rapport by asking open-ended questions such as the who, what, where, when, why, and how. Those questions are crucial to get your prospects to talk about themselves. When that happens, you are now on common ground.

9. *Stay positive:* Avoid negative comments about your company, your product, or the competition. Always take the high road when talking

about your competition. When talking about your competition, don't mention their name. Say things like "the other product doesn't..."

10. *Show your customer the benefits of owning your product:* Explain how it can improve their current situation. Show them savings through percentages. As you climb to the top in selling, most of your prospects want you to quantify how your product will save them money so that they can increase their profits. Statistics are great when doing a presentation. Example: "Mrs. Prospect, by purchasing our product and service agreement, our company figured out that you could save right around 37%, which will go right to your bottom line. How would that work out for you and your company?

11. *Rinse your commission breath.* Customers like to be helped, not sold. If you go for the sale too quickly, most likely they will throw you a series of objections. That is why there has to be a selling process in place. The process is chronological and has to be followed with every prospect.  Salespeople will lose a ton of sales if they go for the close too early. How many times have you personally gone to buy something and walked out because the salesperson asked for the order too soon? That happens for several reasons. One is that the salesperson has not sold anything for a quite some time, just lost a sale earlier in the day, the last prospect they talked to was a lie-down, which means they had a mattress strapped on their back or had the check to buy stapled on their forehead. When in doubt go back to the basics, the road to the sale is paved with steps that are laid down in order. If you vary them, then you have to suffer the consequences.

12. *Use stories:* Show your customer your proof book or evidence manual that other customers have been in the same situation as they

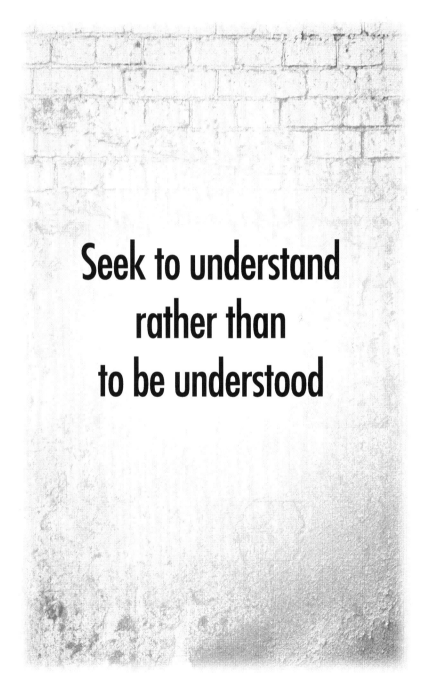

Seek to understand
rather than
to be understood

are. People really do believe more of what they see than what they hear. That is called the *similar-situation close*. Tell your prospect about someone in a similar situation who purchased your product, and how happy they are with you and the product. It is *also called the second-party close,* and you probably have used it without knowing you were using it. Example: You are in a new town, and you ask someone where the best Italian (or whatever you like) restaurant is.

"Do you know of a great Italian restaurant?"

"Oh, sure. You have to go to the one on Broadway and Fifth. It's called Little Italy."

"Is it good?"

"Oh yes, it's the best in town."

"Have you eaten there before?"

"Several times."

"What do you recommend?"

"Get the pasta and veal."

"It's that good?"

"Yep, I wouldn't go anywhere else."

"Great, can I ask you a question, do you own the restaurant?"

"No."

"Then why are you promoting it?"

That is called the second-party close. Powerful—that we would believe a stranger rather than the actual owner.

13. *Don't bore clients:* Get to the point and talk to them about what they want to talk about. Don't vomit all over your customer with unnecessary information. If you do that, you will put them to sleep or

they will throw you a covert objection such as, "I have to go now," and soon it will be, "You have to go now."

14. *Be prepared*: It will help you close more sales. Your prospects time is important as your time is too, be on time and be prepared when you meet your prospect.

15. *Reassure your prospect:* Assure them that they are making the best decision. Don't be afraid to look them in the eye and tell them that they made a great choice.

16. *Prospects like to buy, not be sold:* Don't use old-world selling tactics such as, "Well, we only have one left, you better get this today." We were looking at moving our office and we found the location. The broker called us several times telling us that they had four other prospects looking at the same building. I knew it wasn't true, due to the fact that it had been unoccupied for over six months. I offered them a lower price on top of that. We got the building. I then told the broker, it would be far better to serve your way through the sale instead of lie your way through the sale. They say that buyers are liars. I believe if you ask the right questions for the most part you will hear the truth.

17. *Build the value higher, then the price*: If you don't build value in you, your product, and company then most likely you won't make the sale. Ask for the order.

You show a thermometer with cold being the value which is the bottom, then when you follow the basics, the value climbs higher then the price, which means, they are ready to buy!

18. *Be passionate about what you sell*: Get behind your product so passionately that if your prospect doesn't buy from you, you might have to go into therapy.

You have got to have the feeling from the top of your head to the soles of your feet that what you sell is something they can't live without. We have another company that places businesses at the top of search engines, Google being one of them. When I was presenting it or just talking about it in a normal conversation, I would get so excited and passionate that within minutes I all but had the sale locked up. Sometimes you don't even need to ask for the order, the prospects starts asking you buying questions.

Crazy, isn't it? It's like this book—you can't live without if you want to be the world's greatest closer. Here in this book are the best tips, strategies, and real-world skills you need to become the world's greatest closer. If you get one thing out of this book, get this right here... *Ask and you shall receive.* Now do you see how I can get you excited? I'm so convinced if you don't buy what I sell, you are making a grave mistake. Let's get this wrapped up. Pick up the book or click the mouse and get your credit card out. Are you going to purchase it with a Visa, MasterCard or Amex? That is how you close. Get 100% behind yourself, your product, and your business work place.

Understanding the selling process

You can close a lot more sales if you make a friend.

There are two parts to selling, and if you can grasp this, I can assure you that you will be a very successful salesperson. People don't want to be sold by strangers; people want to buy from people they like and trust. They want to deal with a salesperson who can make a friend, get them to smile, and sell them in a non-confrontational atmosphere. There are two parts to selling and I will break them down for you. The world's greatest closers follow the basics of selling. When you sacrifice the selling process you will lose sales.

Can you sell something without following the basics? Yes. However, the numbers will not be in your favor if you take shortcuts. Don't allow your exceptions to become your norms. With today's overinformed prospects, it seems like everybody wants to cut to the chase and get to the bottom line. Your goal is to take your prospects through the basics of selling so you can increase your own bottom line along with your company's. Shortcuts are pay cuts and the habit of shortcutting the sales process will leave you broke and frustrated. The basics of selling are what will separate you from the pack. Your goal is to bring all of your prospects through the selling process. The benefits for you will be higher profits, happier customers, more referrals, and a fun, rewarding career.

What has happened to the selling process?

With the popularity of the Internet, most prospects do their research before they talk to you or come to your business. That means by the time you see them, they want you to hurry up the process. "I will call you later" happens and the results are disastrous. It happens all the time. We have become an impatient society, haven't we? It seems like fast isn't fast enough and rushing isn't nearly quick

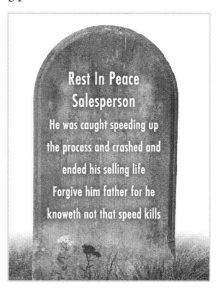

Rest In Peace
Salesperson
He was caught speeding up
the process and crashed and
ended his selling life
Forgive him father for he
knoweth not that speed kills

enough, and if I have to wait that's way too long. If you rush the buying and selling process, then you are rushing yourself to bankruptcy.

If you can learn how to control the selling process, then you can gain control of the sale. Trying to control a customer is called career suicide. Forget it—prospects have too many options today when it comes to purchasing products or services. You can thank the Internet for that.

The Buy-Sell Agreement

The buying process is done early in the selling timeline as illustrated below. If you skip over these steps, then your prospects will feel like they are being sold. Think of selling as if you are talking to people you know. Selling is mostly conversational and *if* you focus on that, you will sell more. There is nothing more deadly to a sale than the word *price* when it comes to making the sale. If you focus on the price during the buying process, it will most likely mean death to the sale and your profits or commissions. You cannot build value while talking price, you must build value to justify the price with your prospect. Believe it or not, price is not the most important thing to your prospect. For some prospects, it's the ability to pay or the emotion of desire that makes them purchase what you sell. It takes skill to stay off price. There are really only two roads a customer takes when purchasing your product. They are either going to want to talk price or let you build the value as you attempt to sell them. Bypassing price is a skill that the world's great closers possess. If you don't bypass price then, about the only thing you can do is drop the price to get your prospect excited to buy. Most of the buying process is about building rapport and lowering your prospect's tension and increasing their belief in you and your product.

Basics — Let's break this down — First steps to the sale

| TENSION | RESPECT | REASONS TO BUY | BELIEF | BUY |

| 1st Imp • Greet • Rapport • Inv • Pres/Demo • Service • Ev • Close • Neg • Close • F/Up |

Now *if you skip steps and go too fast,* that is when *you are going to get in trouble.* Your customer will be raising objections like red flags. If you have twenty closes in your toolbox, most likely they won't matter anyway. Nobody likes to be sold by a high-pressure salesperson who has commission breath.

Shortcuts are pay cuts. You have to follow the steps with every customer and be consistent. That takes sales discipline. One of the biggest problems with sales is that it offers you several opportunities to take shortcuts and be successful. The other problem is that most salespeople don't have someone looking over their shoulder to watch them do their job properly. It's like going to gym—you say to yourself, "Yep, I'm going to do four sets of twelve today." And you do the first two sets of twelve, but now you are getting kind of tired and you think, "Well nobody is going to know that I only did ten reps," and by the last set you say, "Oh six reps are good enough." Who are you fooling? Your body will tell the difference. Your paycheck will show your transparency when you shortcut the sales process. It won't lie to you.

Slow down when you go through the timeline to the sale. Every step is important. If you get the prospect to like you, then they believe you. From there you can start trust selling, which is when the customer lets their guard down and starts listening and engaging in a conversation with you. Do that and your closing ratio will improve dramatically. Selling is all about having a conversation with your prospect and getting them to believe in you and what you are selling. Do that and you will have job security in sales for a lifetime.

Some interesting industry stats that are important to remember

- Seventy percent of the prospects you talk to will buy from you just because they like you.
- Eighty percent of sales are made after the fifth time you ask for the order.
- Sixty percent of people will buy from you if they are a referral.
- Seventy-seven percent of selling is done face-to-face.
- In 1998 there were some 33.56 million salespeople and in 2009 there are 67.66 million salespeople so the sales work force has doubled. This is worldwide.
- In the United States there were 9.7 million salespeople and today there are over 15 million—do you think you have competition?
- The only person you need to worry about is the person you see in the mirror every day.

Bad Habits Lead To the Door Called Failure

Think about the easiest sale you have ever made. The prospect was ready to buy and you didn't have to go through the entire process. What you will find is that the next prospect won't be so easy and you will lose your sale and for the rest of the day, you will be trying to figure out where you went wrong. Follow the steps one by one and remember that each step is a closing step, sort of like stepping stones. Do yourself a favor and remember this to help you close more sales, the most important selling step is the one you are on.

If you ever find yourself struggling in sales, fall back to the basics and I can assure you that your sales will rise again. Look at the best pro teams in sports. The teams that execute the basics seemingly always win. In football, it's blocking, tackling, running, kicking, passing, and team plays. In real life, none of those are headliners in the paper, yet it seems like the teams that execute them win. I have coached hockey for some fifteen years and I had a boy come up to me while we were undefeated with twenty wins and he said, "Hey, coach, when are we going to do some high-end plays?" I responded , "Son, these are the high-end plays!" He said, "But coach, these are just basic plays." "I know they are, but the team who executes the basics will win the championship." Just think for a moment when you were watching TV or were at a sporting event and the pro missed the putt, missed the free throw, threw a ball instead of strike, missed a tackle, or anything of the sort. Normally at the time we swat our forehead and say, "How could he miss that? They make millions and they can't make that shot." It's the basics that count.

Sales Habits - My Friend or My Enemy

The most effective way to break bad habits in sales is to track your performance. Now you have to be honest with yourself and not play the game where you make excuses: they aren't buyers, or they aren't serious, or they are a year away, or they aren't going to buy anyway.

If you track your performance, then you can see where you have failed or succeeded. Let's say you aren't writing up enough orders, but you are seeing enough prospects. Most likely you are missing the rapport-building and investigation stage of selling. Most likely at that point, your presentation of your product will be weakened because you didn't build enough rapport or investigate enough to really find out what your prospect really wants. If you track your performance, then it will easy to adjust and zero in what you need to change and improve on. Don't change to change, change so that you can profit from change.

Change Your Habits

The world's great closers know that good habits will lead them to the door called success and bad habits will lead them to failure. There are so many salespeople who had the talent to be the best salespeople yet never could get to the top of their game. If you have lousy habits, then you will have lousy earnings, I assure you. Your habits control your thinking and how you act on them. Habits are friends at first, but soon they become your master. When you try to break them and use will power, most likely you are setting yourself up for failure. Remember if you break a habit, then there will be a void in your brain. Your mind is like a memory chip, it stores the old habits and ways of thinking. If you don't replace a bad habit with a good habit, soon you will be falling back to your old ways. Your habits will determine your future, not the current job you have.

You have to unlock the doors or remove the chains that have you anchored down. Break free by first recognizing what bad habits you have. Don't be afraid of the truth. You will either run to it or flee from it. The quicker you come to the truth, the less pain you have to go through in life. Change is hard, change is tough, and if you don't change you will die a slow death. Then you will play the should game, I should have done this, I should have done that, I should have changed; soon you will *should* all over yourself. What a shame to waste a life on things that you could have controlled or changed. Why wait? Just do it now! As a matter of fact, if there is something you have been putting off for some time, put the book down, get up, and do it right now. Okay, put the book down and just do it!

Tips to Help You Develop Good Habits and Become a Great Closer

1. Recognize you have a bad habit first—write it down in your journal or in a safe place.

2. Visualize the change in your mind—see it so you can be it—think it so you will do it.

3. Start with small changes—don't go for an extreme makeover.

4. Go for consistency first, don't attempt to do everything in one day. Start small, like exercising. If you say I am going to run a mile a day and you fail at it—the next day, just walk around the block or something of that nature. You don't have to do a marathon. Build yourself up slowly each day by doing the same thing every day.

5. Find a support group or a friend to help and encourage you. This really works for accountability and support.

6. Set your own goals accordingly; place them just a bit out of reach. Write them down, review them daily, and keep them in sight.

7. If you fail at changing your habit, don't give up. Find out why you failed and then adapt and start again. Life is really about start-and-stop programs, most people start but stop. If at first you don't succeed try, try again. But it doesn't make sense to do the same thing over and over and expect a different result. That is called insanity. *Adapt* and start again.

8. Don't ever play the *should* game. People constantly say, I should do this, I should do that, I should do this; soon you'll go right back to where you started.

9. Decide to change and then commit to change.

10. Leverage your mind into believing that if you change, the change will profit you both personally and professionally. If you stay where you are, it will cost you a fortune or your life.

You were put on this earth to serve and help people, and you have the power to make the right choices or the wrong ones. The cost of not changing should be higher than the cost to change. People won't change until the pain of staying the same is greater than the pain of

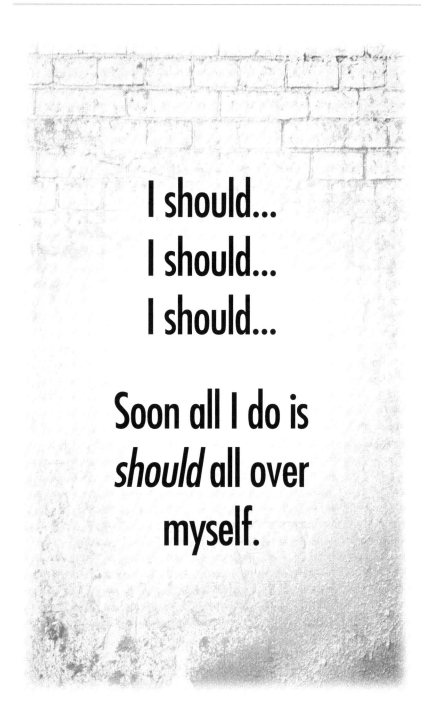

I should...
I should...
I should...

Soon all I do is
should all over
myself.

change. I have used leverage thinking for years. I look at it like a scale where if I stay here, this is what it's going to cost me. If I change and come over here, these are the benefits of changing. Take out a sheet of paper and on the left side, write out what will happen to you if you stay where you are and don't change.

. . . .

"The pain of regret weighs tons, the pain of change only weighs the pain of discipline to change" —Jim Rohn

What do I need to be The World's Greatest Closer?

Traits That Develop Champions!

There probably isn't a career more fraught with disappointment than being a salesperson. The word no to a salesperson is like a disease that you don't want to catch. You will hear it over and over and you must learn how to handle it and get over it. You can't spend your golden minutes worrying about why you didn't make the sale, if you do the days will pass you by. Every great closer possesses certain traits.

The World's Greatest Closer Has:

- The will to win and ask for the order—Just ask for it—just close it!
- The skills to handle objections—Practice every day, because you are going to hear them forever.
- The ability to handle and overcome rejection—Let it go—say *next*.
- Such a strong belief in what they sell that if their prospect doesn't buy it, they would have to go into therapy to get over it—LOL.
- The ability to speak on their feet and handle any type of questions that are thrown at them.

- The will to train, train, train, and train to insure consistent performance.
- The ability to listen to self-help programs to build up their skills.
- The world's greatest closer has the best damn positive attitude.
- The confidence to close anyone.
- The experience to know that *no* means *not yet*.
- The understanding to never allow the underachievers of selling to bring them down.
- The time every day to polish their vocabulary.
- The good sense to practice their selling scripts.
- Persistence.
- The skills of a great listener—They listen to what the client needs. It's almost impossible to listen your way out of sales, but you sure can talk your way out of a sale if you don't know what the client needs.
- Shuts up when they ask for the order.
- Follows the road to the sale, which is paved with the stepping stones of the buying and selling process.
- Knows that proper preparation prevents poor performance.
- Has *faith,* which is the pillar of all great salespeople—in your darkest times of sales, fall back and look up because the answers are right above you.

I have studied and spoken to thousands of salespeople and you see a pattern of traits that they possess. You can have the above traits, but you will have to work for them. CANI is a acronym that stands for Constant And Never-ending Improvement which was derived from the Japanese word *kaizen.* Selling and closing are a lifelong journey, and if you educate and apply yourself, then nothing should stop you from closing more sales. Learn more, earn more.

Prospects and customers don't like it when salespeople use old-world

F *Focus*

A *And*

C *Channeled*

E *Enthusiasm*

C *Can do*

H *Help*

A *Attitude*

N *Never give up*

G *God*

E *Everyone Can*

tactics, which are primarily high pressure. When prospects feel pressure, objections come up. There are times when you can overcome those objections by dropping your price. If you are on commission though, it will be costly. My best selling tip is to follow the basics with every customer. Pick a path and follow it. The selling path is paved with the basic selling steps.

Why do I have to follow them?

There are two reasons people spend money: logic and emotion. When customers use logic, they tend to negotiate a harder bargain, because the value hasn't been placed higher than the price. Oh, sure, your prospect wants to buy your product, but they want to make sure they get the best price and deal. At this point of the sale, all you can really do is work the numbers and most likely you will have to drop your numbers which could cost you commission.

Can't I take shortcuts and still sell?

Yes, but I wouldn't recommend it!

Value-Based Selling

Value-based selling is best way to sell a prospect, because when a buyer perceives the value to be higher than the price, you are ready to close. You will make more commission. Your sale will be easier to close. The best way to value-sell is to determine exactly what your customer wants and needs, and his motivation to buy your product. Think of selling as being a detective—you can't prosecute someone unless you have the evidence, and selling is the same way. Most salespeople miss sales because they missed the most important steps to the sale. They never found out their customer's hot buttons. If you don't know their hot buttons, or their wants and needs, then you will have trouble building your sale. Miss those steps and you probably have a house of cards.

The best way to determine what your prospect's needs are is to ask them questions that will lead you to the next step in the selling process. Don't assume what your customer needs, as that will cause all kinds of havoc and a disconnect. They may give you some excuse that they have to go—they are on their way somewhere else.

ASK AND YOU
SHALL RECEIVE!

CHAPTER EIGHT

Change, Adjust, and Manage

Change or Die Right Now

If you don't change, your career in sales will die. People pick up books for different reasons: reference, information, knowledge, improvement, overcoming fear, or in your case, change. Nobody likes to stay in one place too long, especially with income level. If you want to change your income, then you have to change your skills. It takes great skills to pay the bills. People generally don't like change though. I know people who hate change. They would rather take personal beatings then change. People think of change like getting sued or having a tooth pulled. They don't like it.

Yet most people like more change in their pocket, don't they? I would suspect that most people change their clothes daily. Most shower each day, most do something different each day. It's just that people don't like being told what or when to change. The need to change should be at the top of your list. If you want to earn more money, you need to change your skills and your work habits. The reasons people won't change could take up the rest of the book. Often people talk about change, but when it comes to putting their money where their mouth is, that disappears. *Big-talker-no-action* salespeople are in every industry. They talk a great game, but when it comes to walking the talk, they are crippled with excuses.

How to Conquer Change

Another reason people don't change is that they are led astray by the easy way. They allow too many outside influences to control their thought patterns. They become shaped by the world they live in. If you are going to change, then you have to change that right away. You can't let the outside world influence your change compass. If you do, the cost is almost too much to pay. Time will be the most expensive cost to pay.

People don't change because they don't slow down to allow change to catch them. So time passes on and on. Then one day you wake up and say, where did the time go? Understand this about change, it's hard, it takes time, and you have to see the profit's of changing first before you change. In other words, you have to see the outcome of the change. If you can't see the profit's, then you won't pay the price to change.

"People won't change until the pain of same is greater than the pain of change." —Dave Ramsey

If you can learn how to leverage your mind, you can leapfrog ahead of your current income and place in life. If you stay where you are, think about how much it will cost you. What will you be missing? What will it cost you to stay there? Can you afford it? How will it affect your life to stay where you are? What will it cost your family? Who will be affected the most?

Is there risk involved? Job security is risk taking.

Risk and fear seem to be joined at the hip of failure. With change and growth come more rewards and risks. You can't be afraid of risks. We know that there are practical reasons why you won't change. There could be a company you own, family, homes, and so on, but does that mean that you are paralyzed? No. I have often lived by the idea that job security is risk taking.

What if you fail, though? Get up and dust your butt off and put your right foot in front of your left and get going again! You can always get up and get going again, can't you? Think of how many failures you had in sports and life. If you played sports, did you always get a hit, did you always score a touchdown? Did you always get every answer right on a test? Mistakes don't make people, people make mistakes! The defeats in life are many, but you can always learn from your defeats. The defeats toughen you up and if you are a determined person, you will rebound from your failures

It's okay to take calculated risks. Be prepared and have a plan. Follow the old mantra—*proper planning prevents poor performance.* You have a choice: to change or to stay the same. Come up with your core values and live by them. Don't negotiate with them. Don't allow the negaholics of today's world to spill their negativity all over you. You don't need to gain agreement with a negaholic's opinion.

Slow down so you can speed up

Change will happen if you slow down a bit. I know that goes against the popular principles in life. If you don't slow down, then you die a slow death. You have to stop and eat, don't you? You have to slow down and put gas in your car, don't you? You have to slow down and go the grocery store, don't you? You have to slow down and work out, don't you? People spend far too much time just going through life instead of growing through life. The path to growth is easy to say and hard to do, but it's worth the effort, because the returns are forever.

Instead of becoming a secret agent, become a change agent

Learn how to change from being negative to positive. Change from saying "I can't" to "I can" from now on. Change the habit of blaming others or finding fault in others. Understand you can control what you can control. Look for good in others. Change from the habit of talking down about others and instead talk them up. Change from the habit of being closed-minded to being open-minded. The best way to become open-minded is to listen to others. Change from the habit of "why me" to the habit of "I can make it happen." Change from the habit of "I should" because soon you will be saying I should do this, I should do that, and soon you will have done nothing of consequence. Change is good, change is constant, change is challenging, and those who change the fastest often win in life.

If you are not of the mindset of proving why people should change, and buy your product, most likely you will be changing careers often. You are a change agent. Your mission to commission is to prove to them that what you sell is something they can't live without.

Change one thing right now.Whatever it is, change it right now, if it means working out, making an extra call, finishing a report, cleaning up, getting up, practicing your skills, calling a customer, making one extra visit for the day, prospecting, just get up and do it now. Action is priceless isn't it? That's how you change, you take action towards your goal.

Winners do all the activities that losers hate to do!

Count My Days — I Only Have So Many

If you are blessed to live to seventy-five, that means you will have lived 3900 weeks. Take your age and multiply it by fifty-two weeks.

T *Time*

I *Is*

M *My*

E *Enemy*

That's the amount of weeks you have lived so far. The remaining time is what you have left if you make it to seventy-five. Can you afford to wait? Do you know what the biggest problem is in life when it comes to doing things? Here it is. People know what to do, what they don't know is *why* they don't do what they should do! Start doing more instead of talking more, and more will get done. It's almost too easy isn't it? Look around you and observe how many people you know that didn't make it to thirty years old, forty years old, fifty years old, sixty years old, If I were you I would get going right now. Dump your *wait till tomorrow* attitude today.

Be very careful of time leaks—they are all over the place. Look at how you approach your day and find the lost minutes that seem to be stolen from you. Think about how much time people spend killing time at work or during their day.

"If you kill time, you should be arrested for murder."
—Zig Ziglar

Long lunches are a waste unless you are with a client. Think about how much time you need to warm up your day. Do you have to have coffee, visit other departments, play online a bit, read the paper, gossip, deal with your home problems which follow you to work. Instead you should be focusing on activities that will bring you great results.

The sure way to getting fired is to give up when you get to the middle of the month and say, "Oh well, this month is over, I can get them next month." The salespeople who say that are weak, pathetic, mealy-mouthed quitters who are hitting below average with amazing accuracy. The first hour of your workday sets the pace for the day. If you start slow, doesn't it seem like the whole day is slow? Before you know it, it's time to leave and the day is over, never to be here again. How many days can you afford to waste?

Look out for time killers — which one is killing you?

1. Too many coffee breaks
2. Procrastination
3. No sales plan for the day
4. Too much time making sales calls instead of sales
5. Long lunches
6. Showing up to work around ten or eleven a.m.
7. Unorganized paperwork
8. Majoring in minor activities instead of major activities
9. Internet surfing—email, texting
10. Smoke breaks
11. Gossip – spells GoPiss halfway backwards! Go Figure, if you can't say something nice, be quiet!
12. Killing time
13. Personal issues
14. Looking for files or paperwork
15. Disorganization

Look at the above and pick several of them to change, and just do it. Don't put life on layaway; just do something now to improve. Don't wait for the right time to improve; it won't ever come along, just do it now!

Time Killers

I was doing some sales training for a large Fortune 500 company and management wanted me to observe how their salespeople spent their day. The company knew they had the right product but couldn't seem to improve their profits. For the most part, the salespeople spent more of the day wasting time than working.

Time Killers

- Salespeople showing up late to work
- Salespeople came to work to break then work
- Salespeople spent too much time in the WFL (What's For Lunch Bunch)
- Stood around talking to other employee's
- Gossiping
- Water breaks or vendor tackling
- Personal phone calls
- Extended stay at lunch
- Too many ten minute breaks that went to thirty minute breaks
- Searching for files because they are disorganized
- Personal shopping'
- Web surfing is now a new work sport
- Texting to friends
- Emails
- Personal work at work
- Social networking
- Smoking
- Talking too much
- Boring meetings
- Write your own in here _____

If you got rid of the above, don't you think you would be more productive? What if people just went to work to actually work? Companies would be more productive and profitable because everybody would be working. How often we have heard, time is money. Why would you put off what you need to do today?

It's time for more doing than talking. Take out a pad of paper today and write out five activities you need to accomplish today.

1. Review game plan for month
2. Make fifty phone calls
3. Two appointments—Visit two clients today.
4. Send out twenty emails
5. Ask for two referrals

After you have completed number one, then move to number two, if all you do today is get to number three, then number four becomes number one the next day. Do that and you will be more productive right away.

Someday is not a day in the week.

How many times have you said, "Oh, I will get to that someday." Someday is not a day in the week. Someday turns into tomorrow and that turns into next week, then next month, then next year and soon it becomes never. Procrastination and someday are joined at the hip of failure. Both are a salesperson's greatest enemy. The best method to cure procrastination is to put procrastination off to tomorrow and do it now. When you want to get things done, repeat the words, do it now, do it now, do it now, do it now, and then get up and do it now.

Manage time or management of activities

You will always hear people say, "I don't have the time," or "I ran out of time," or "I wish I could have better time management skills." Nobody can manage time, it is impossible to stop the clock, or add time to it. It doesn't matter if you are Gates, Turner, Buffet, or Trump, none of them have the ability to stop time or add time to their precious twenty-four hours they get each day. The difference for them is that they know how to get the most out of the time they have. No matter how much money you have, you can't buy more time. Most salespeople who are hitting average in sales complain about time. Their main problem is that they are killing time. If you are a salesperson killing time, then you should be arrested for murder.

86,400

The above number represents the seconds in a day. Every one of us gets the same amount, but not everyone gets the most use out of the 86,400 seconds. There are several time killers in the day, and if you can figure out how to be more productive, then the time killers will move on to another salesperson. You are given the day but once, and if you don't get the most out of your day, then you have to return your minutes. Real life doesn't have a rollover-minute plan. You have one day, and it's this day. Time is precious. The young want to burn it too fast, and the old, want to save it and get more out of it. There are people who seemingly can get what seems to be seven days out of one day and then there are others who get one day out of seven.

1440

This is the number of minutes you have every day. If you don't have a game plan for each day, then the day is going to plan you. Like most normal people, you probably sleep a third of the day, so that leaves you with 960 minutes, of which 480 minutes are used for work and you still have 480 left. It comes down to having your day planned out. In most sales businesses, the month seems to come together in the last week of the month, because most salespeople fill their month in the last week.

CHAPTER NINE

Objections, and What to do About Them

You will always hear objections. I wish I had kept count of how many salespeople told me that they had heard these scripts before. You don't want to go through your career struggling to overcome these objections, do you?

Prospect Scripts:

- I need to think about it
- We just started looking
- We can't make a decision
- It's more then we can afford
- We need to compare and shop
- Give us some time, we will get back to you
- Thanks for your time, but we are not ready today
- Thanks, we just want to get some information
- Today we are just looking and not buying
- We are going to call around

- I don't think we can do anything right now
- Call me back in a few weeks
- I will take a brochure if you have one

All the above are your prospect's scripts. Most salespeople go their entire career never knowing how to handle those objections. When you hear those objections and you don't attempt to overcome them, the results could be fatal to your career. What most salespeople end up doing is chasing the false objection that their prospects sold them. When a prospect says no, that means they are selling you on not buying. Closers don't buy objections; they skillfully handle and then overcome them until they close their sale.

The real sale doesn't start until you hear the word no.

It's almost like sports, when you think about it. There are three seasons that most sports teams endure during the year, they have preseason, the real season, then the playoffs. Think of selling and closing the same way. You warm up on the way to your call, then you play the game, which is the basics, and when you hear the word no, that's when the playoffs start.

Signs that your customer isn't interested in you or your product anymore

They start looking at their watch. They are looking for a way out. They ask questions like:

- How long are you open to?
- Do you normally cover this territory?
- We really need to go and think about it.
- We are just looking.
- When can you leave?

- Is your manager here?
- We just started looking, can we be left alone?
- Can I get your business card (which is dismissal slip to a customer)?
- They look at each other like, "Hey, how can we get out of here?"

The way to speak to objections.

Untrained salespeople talk too much, and that's what gets them in trouble. You have to learn how to ask questions so that you can stay connected to your customer and build value in your time and presentation with your customer. If they don't know you then their trust level is down, the tension level is high, and their belief in you is down. This is why most sales are missed: the salesperson didn't change those emotions.

Can I tell my way through a sale or *ask* my way?

You can't tell your way through a sale, you have to ask your way. Too often salespeople think that if they give their customer too much information, sooner or later the prospect will grab onto a life preserver and say, "Yes that's what I am interested in." If the salesperson does all the talking then the customer will become disengaged or disconnected from you and the selling process. Just ask!

Selling is no different from any other profession, there has to be a foundation. Just because you have the best product doesn't insure your success when it comes to selling or closing your deal. The foundation of selling is the questions you ask so that you can sell your product. I can't stress that enough. If you have been in sales then most likely you have been taught that when you ask for the order you should shut up. One of the main problems with salespeople is that they do most of the talking. Think of today's generation. Most people can't even focus on one thing at a time. If you are talking too much then your customer will be turned off. When that happens, you can expect your prospect to start looking around, looking at their watch, asking you how long this will take or when can we talk next. At that point, the sale is most likely lost. The objections will be so big that there really isn't much of a chance to make your sale. If you talk too much then you won't be connected with your customer's needs, wants, or motivation.

The Three Most Powerful Questions

These three questions will be with you forever. They are the foundation of selling and will take you to heights of sales and income if you take the time to master them. The questions are great ways to handle objections.

The Three Types of questions
1. Yes Questions
2. Either/Or—choice questions
3. Open-ended Questions

Yes Questions

Yes questions are aimed at getting minor commitments along the way. Closing the sale is a process; it's not where you hold your breath until your face turns red and then you ask a closing question. Yes questions help you build value throughout the selling process. The end result will be that your closing ratios will increase. If you can get your prospect to say yes at key times, then when you get ready to close, you're just asking another question. Wouldn't that help you close more sales?

Think of it like this. If you deposit a series of yes questions through-out the process, then you can withdraw them at the end of the selling process. Wouldn't it be great to have your customer say yes to you more often? Your job would be a lot easier, wouldn't it? Isn't it great that you are learning to sell more by reading this book? Selling can be fun, right? These questions will be a great addition to your bag of tools, right? They will help with objections, won't they?

Wouldn't it be nice to get your customers or prospects more involved in the sale? Couldn't these questions get your customer more involved in the sale? Don't your prospect's eyes start to glaze over when you talk too much? Don't they become disconnected from you and your sales process? Have you noticed that I have been using the yes questions at the beginning of each statement? I should move them around, shouldn't I? I did move them around, didn't I? They are at the end of the sentences now, aren't they? That was another one, wasn't it? You could do this too, couldn't you? With some practice, wouldn't it be nice to put these questions in the middle of the sentence? I just did that, didn't I? It's getting repetitive, isn't it? I should stop, shouldn't I? I'm done, aren't I? If you get your prospect to say yes several times during the selling process, then the close will be much easier, won't it? I can't stop, can I? When I am performing at my large seminars, I normally have an attendee count how many yeses I can get in six to eight minutes. It usually ends up being about 140 yes questions.

Salespeople think that sometimes the customer will say, "that's what I am looking for" or "that's what I need." Think about all the times you have bought products or services. Most likely you asked questions, didn't you? When a salesperson asks the right questions, prospects feel like that the salesperson is more interested in finding out what they need than trying to sell them what they don't need.

It's hard for you to listen your way out of sale, but you can talk your way out of a sale. I like it when prospects say, "Oh, that salesperson is a great listener." That's because the salesperson asked questions and then kept quiet while their prospect answered. Questioning is an art that can be mastered and used quickly. This chapter is one of those chapters that you should read over and over again. No matter what you sell, these questions will help you sell more products or services right away.

What is a yes question?

A yes question is when you take certain words and add a positive ending:

- Shouldn't it?
- Couldn't it?
- Wouldn't it?
- Won't it?
- Can't it?
- Isn't it?
- Doesn't it?
- Aren't you?
- Can't you?
- Haven't they?
- Won't you?
- Eh? (that's my Canadian tie-down)

Using these kinds of words will help you gain a series of minor commitments throughout your sale. The key to using these words is that you have to space them out throughout the process. If you don't, you will sound like a scripted salesperson. Practice using them throughout your day and look for any opportunity to get a yes.

Lets break down the two types of yes questions that will help you become the world's greatest closer!

Two Types of Yes Questions

1. Tie-Down Yes Questions—the definition of a tie-down question is when you know the answer and you confirm it with your prospect. If you have done a proper investigation of your prospect's wants and needs, these questions will help you.

- "Mr. Customer, didn't you say that this product will help you solve your company's problems?"
- "Wouldn't this allow production to run smoother?"
- "Isn't it great that this will add money to your bottom line?"
- "This sure looks great, doesn't it?"
- "That's an important feature, isn't it?"
- "Won't this help your company out?"
- "We should write it up, shouldn't we?"
- "You did see the value, didn't you?"
- "Wouldn't this improve your sales?"

2. Tag-On Yes Questions—The yes questions remain the same except when your prospect says something and you can confirm it, then you use the yes questions. The more yeses you get, the higher your closing ratio will be. Listen carefully to what your prospect says and when you hear an opportunity to get them to say yes to you, then use the tag-on yes question.

- **Example:** Mrs. Customer says, "Oh, I like the design of your product."
- **Salesperson** (Tag on to their sentence): "Yes, it does look good, doesn't it?" (Don't forget to nod your head)
- **Mrs. Customer:** "Yes it does, I like the way it looks."
- **Salesperson:** "It's nice, isn't it?"
- **Mrs. Customer:** "Yes."
- **Mr. Prospect:** "I like how this product can fit into our plans, and I can see it saving us some money."

- **Salesperson**: "Yes, those are both important to you, aren't they?"

If you can get a series of mini-commitments then your closing ratio will improve. Don't go for the one big closing question. When salespeople try to use one big question, that places too much pressure on your prospect. At that point, the objections will be too much to overcome.

Practice using your questions each day until they become natural. At some point they will become part of your everyday vocabulary. It makes sense, doesn't it?

Either/Or Questions

If you want to be the world's greatest closer, then you must master this type of question. There are other names for this question such as choice question, multiple-choice, or option question.

Questions will help you close more sales right now. The worst thing you can do when you close is to ask an open question such as this.

- SP: "So Mr. and Mrs. Prospect, what do you think of our product?"
- Prospect: "Well, it's okay. We really aren't that sure though, so why don't you get back to us?"

Use these instead:

- WGC: "Well, Mr. and Mrs. Prospect, did you want to take delivery of our product on Wednesday or Thursday?"
- WGC: "Mr. Prospect, did you want to pay by check or credit card?"
- WGC. "Mrs. Prospect, should we set up the delivery date on Friday or Saturday?"

- WGC: "Ok this sounds great, did you want to put that on a purchase order or did you want to write a check out right now?"

You give your customer a buying choice because you gave them an option question. The either/or question is the best closing question and will improve your closing ratio practically overnight. Remember, one of two things will happen when you use this question. One, you will close your sale, or two, an objection might come up. Be prepared to handle the objection.

The telephone is one of the world's greatest closer's tools and the either/or question is like the backstop or foothold of your conversation. If you never master the skills of using the telephone, then you will need more than a casino of luck to close sales. Salespeople are either phone ninjas or phone wimps.

Setting the appointment is almost like closing a sale. If you can't get in front of your prospects, then it's going to be tough to close sales. You have to get face time with prospects or belly-to-belly selling. A lot of salespeople don't like using the phone. Why? Because they don't have the skills they need, and they struggle. If you can't set appointments—good luck to you. Most prospects have gatekeepers and the only way to get through to them is by having great phone skills. When setting an appointment, don't use weak scripts such as:

- "Would it be okay if I stop by?" "No."
- "Can I come by later?" "No."
- "When can we meet?" "Never."

Use scripts like this:

- "Would Wednesday or Thursday be better for you?"

- "I have an opening at 2:15 or 2:45, which time would be better for you?"
- "Can I stop by today or tomorrow?"
- "Can you come in right now or a little bit later on?"
- "I can come over right now or a little bit later on, what works for you?"

Plus use the fifteen/forty-five rule when setting appointments. The percentages of your prospect showing up can improve up to thirty plus percent! Example: I have an opening at 2:15 or 2:45. Which one would be better for you? One more tip, have your prospect always write down the set appointment. There isn't anything worse than waiting for your appointment to show up, and they don't. I can't tell you how many times I have seen this in a sales department. I would then ask the salesperson, "Where is your appointment?" "I don't know." "Well get on the phone and call them!" There is nothing worse than hearing this from your prospect, "We already bought." Every time you lose a sale, you pay a fine. The fine is the amount of commission you would have made.

You can investigate, set appointments, build rapport, and close with this question. Be careful though, if you use too many of these, it will sound like you are interrogating. The best selling tip about using the questions is to mix them up. If you master the questions, then you will possess a strong selling skill foundation. Without the questions, you will struggle in sales. You must ask your way through the sale.

Open Ended Questions

Building rapport is one of the most important steps to the sale, because prospects don't want to buy from strangers or someone they don't like or trust. If you miss this valuable step, then most likely you will miss more sales then you make. Prospects lack trust in people they don't like or believe in. When that happens, they throw up objections, and most sales-people can't overcome them. People want to buy from people they trust. The world's greatest closers make friends before they go for the close. If you go into your sale with a *serve* attitude instead of a *sell* attitude, naturally your closing ratio will improve dramatically. I can't tell you how many times I personally have gone out to buy something and walked out because the salesperson didn't build some sort of rapport. Think of purchases you have made and why you bought. You bought from somebody who built rapport with you. Learn how to slow your prospect down by asking open-ended questions which are meant to build trust, lower tension, and increase your prospect's belief in you, your product, and your company.

Examples of open-ended, common-ground questions:

- Where do you guys normally go on your vacations?
- Who is your favorite sports team?
- What school do your kids go to?
- Where do you live?
- How long have you worked in your current position?
- What did you do before you got to this position?
- When normally will you be using our product?
- What do you think it will mean to you and your company?
- What do you do in your off times from work?
- What kind of sports are you into?
- Where do you go and workout?

If you can get your prospect on common ground, then you will lower their tension and increase their belief in you and what you are selling. Sales isn't all about commission breath. It's about establishing a conversation outside of selling, and then bringing it back to what you are selling. The key to building rapport is to be interested in your prospect instead of being more interesting. Why is that? People like to talk about themselves and if all you do is talk about yourself and your product, you won't become the world's greatest closer.

Get people to open up by getting them to talk about themselves. It is hard to do that if you don't like talking to people. I can't tell you how many salespeople I have met who actually don't like asking questions about people. Most of them should go back to being order takers. Talk people, then talk product. Your closing ratio will improve.

Questions by George:

- Why did you buy this book?
- What would it mean to you to be able to improve your closing ratio?
- What would you do with the extra money?
- Where would you go?
- Who is going to help you then?
- When would you go—soon or down the road a bit?
- It would be fun wouldn't it?

Now did you see how I built rapport? Did you see how I used all three questions in the above sentence? I used the yes, open-ended, and either/or question, didn't I? I just used another yes question, didn't I? Wouldn't the above questions help you?

Body Language and How It Will Help You Close More Sales

The 7/38/55 combination—how does it affect me? There are three ways to communicate with your prospect when it comes to a person. The secret here—this is what the best closers do, is to have the three methods in sync.

Seven percent of how you communicate are the words you use.

Thirty-eight percent of how you communicate is your tone and inflection; in other words, how you modulate your voice—up, down, low, high, excited, half dead.

Fifty-five percent of how you communicate is by using your body language—if you add 7-38-55 together it adds up to 100%. So what does this mean to you? When you are using your yes questions, get in the habit of nodding your head. It's amazing that when you get your head bobbing up and down, your prospect's head will move up and down. It takes a bit of practice and before you know it, you will have more prospects saying yes than ever before.

How to handle no and overcome it.

No means not now. No means tell me more to say yes. No means I want to say yes, but I need more information to say yes. No is two thirds of yes. No is just a yellow caution light. No is word you will hear for the rest of your life.

Most salespeople really never ask for the order, because they are afraid of hearing the dreaded word NO. No means that you are closer to the sale. No means your prospect doesn't know enough to say yes. At this point you have to discover what the true objection is. If you don't have the skills to flush it out, then you won't be able to close your sale. A majority of salespeople who don't investigate properly think that if they drop the price, that will excite their prospect. Quite the contrary, price isn't always the main objection. If you have been disciplined and followed the selling process, then most likely it will come down to three areas. Everybody wants a good deal, most prospects want to make sure they can afford it.

Most objections fall into three categories. It really doesn't matter what you sell, whether it's service or goods, Prospects want to make sure they are making the right decisions. Fear stops prospects from making good decisions, and you will find out that prospects will use stall tactics on you. You will always hear these objections as long as you are in sales:

Objections

- I need to think it over.
- We aren't sure.
- Can I have your business card?
- We will get back to you.
- We are going to compare.
- I have to talk to my spouse.
- Need to check it out with my accountant.
- We are just looking today.
- We don't need help, but we will call you over if needed.
- Our company has to review it.
- We are in the discovery process.
- Can you follow up with us in time?
- Send me some information.
- This is a big decision and I am going to have to sleep on it.
- This is the first product we have looked at.
- We never buy at the first place.
- I have a friend in the business.
- Can you just give me a brochure?

There are countless objections, and the good news is that you don't have to have several scripts to overcome objections. I can't tell you how many salespeople I have met who tell me they were never professionally trained to handle objections or overcome them. Not learning this skill is probably the costliest mistake of your career. If you don't learn how to overcome objections, then it will be hard for you to become the world's greatest closer. This one skill can lead you to a very rewarding selling career.

Group All Objections in These categories — Decision, Deal, or Budget

If you can master the skill of placing all objections into these three categories, I can assure you that closing will become easier for you. You can improve your sales right now by learning this skill. This is what turns average salespeople into the world's greatest closers.

Six easy steps to overcoming objections:

1. Non-confrontational response
2. Confirm need or service
3. Identify true objection
4. Paraphrase objection
5. Isolate objection
6. Close on objections

When you are ready to close your deal or sale, you have to ask a closing question, and that will bring you a few responses. If you have followed the steps to the sale, most likely you will hear yes more than no. There will be times when your prospect says no to you and I will break the six steps down.

Closing the Sale or Losing the Sale:

Salesperson: (Close) "Well it seems like the products I have presented are just what you needed. Are you going to use a purchase order or will you be writing a check?"

Prospect: "Well, right now I would like to take some time and think about it."

Step 1—Acknowledge. "I understand, I know what you mean. That's great." You can use any of these when a customer says no to you. The key is not to get mad or show your cards when they say no. Remember not to take no personally. They are saying no—not never.

Step 2—Confirm needs or services. "Well, you do see the value in our products don't you? It will work out for you, won't it? It sure will save your company a lot of money, won't it? It sure sounded good, didn't it? You do like the color, don't you? It sure will make your business run smoother, won't it?" The strategy right now is to get your prospect to say yes to you and get a minor commitment from them. You have to remember they said no to your closing question. By using the first step, you take the fight out of them, then you come back and confirm the need by getting them to say yes to you. All of sudden you have turned them somewhat around.

Step 3—Identifying the true objection and flushing it out. Make sure you use an *either or question*, don't use an open-ended question.

Salesperson, "Just so I understand, is it the product, the model, the equipment, service, or the price that you need to think about? If you give them an overload answer they will have to pick one. If you come back with what most salespeople say (is it the price?), your prospect will respond with a conditioned response which is normally *no*. For years people have been asked the same questions over and over so it is normal for them to say no. It's as simple as when you walk into a department store and the salesperson says to you, "Can I help you?" What is your normal response? "No, we are just looking."

In most retail closing situations, it normally comes down to the price. Now, if you have missed your steps to the sale then several different types of objections will come up. This is a very challenging sale to close. Why is that? Because at that point the objections seem to grow so big that the only way to overcome them is to pressure your prospect which is not a good thing to do or you have to drop your price. If you are paid on commission then you are taking a pay cut. I have often heard that shortcuts are pay cuts. Let's say your prospect says it's the price, now is your opportunity to paraphrase the objection.

Step 4—Paraphrasing is bringing the objection around to where you have the selling advantage again. Master these three scripts and you will close more sales right now.

a. Financial or money objections: "Sounds to me like you just want to make sure it fits in your needs and budget, am I right?" or, "It really sounds like you and your company want to make sure it fits in the monies you have budgeted for this purchase, am I right?"

b. Can't make a decision: "Do you need to sleep on it, pray on it, think about it, need more time, check with friends, call your accountant?" or "Sounds to me like you want to make a good decision, am I right?" or "I appreciate that you need to think about it or sleep on it, and it sounds like you just want to make the right decision, am I right?"

c. Prospect is looking for a good deal: They say, "Well, we want to look around and make sure we are doing the right thing, or they say that this is our first place so we want to check out some other places like yours. Come back with this: "It really sounds to me like you want to make sure you are getting a good deal, am I right? Isn't a good deal purchasing the products you need at a competitive price from me and our company, which will take care of you long after the sale has been made?" Bonus statement, "Let me ask you this, why would you shop elsewhere and settle for less?"

Step 5—Isolating objections. This is probably the most critical point of closing your sale. If you make mistakes on all the other steps, this step will save you and help you close your sale. Isolating objections prevents your prospects from bringing up other objections. If you don't isolate objections then others will keep coming up, and it will cost you more than your commissions.

At some point you have to have the courage and skills to use this step. It takes guts and a lot of heart but it will pay you back if you use it. The prospect says, "We want to make sure we can afford it and we are on budget." Come back with this, "Other than that, Mr. and Mrs. Prospect, is there any other reason why we couldn't wrap it up right now?" If it's an equipment or feature objection, isolate the objection by saying this script: "Other than that feature, is there any other reason why we couldn't wrap it up right now?" The good point here is that most prospects are flexible. Don't get cornered into thinking that they have to have exactly what they want. The key words in isolating objections are these two words "Other than." If you lose control and you are near the close, just come back and say this: "Other than that, is there any other reason why we couldn't finish this up right now?" Do yourself a favor and master these sixteen words!

You can always change certain words around when closing. However, the more disciplined you are in your scripts the more confidence you will have behind your words.

CHAPTER TEN

How to Let it Go and Move On

. . . .

Now what? They said no to me—how do I get over it?

How you handle rejection is a choice.

A salesperson will hear the word no many times. The world's greatest closers can overcome the word and the emotion. No is part of the selling game and though you may not ever get used to it, you have to get over it and move on to the next prospect or sale. One no can cost you several sales and tons of money. Think about how many times you hear the word no and how many times it has ruined your next call or prospect visit.

No is not the end of the world, no is not the end of the day, and no is not the final word in sales. No means not now, it doesn't mean never. Salespeople take no personally too many times. Why didn't they buy? Because the salesperson didn't convince them to buy. It's that simple. Shortcuts are fatal to a salesperson's career. Taking the word no personally is like a disease with no cure. It's deadly to your paycheck. You can't take the word no personally.

No means not now—no doesn't mean never...Don't take the word no personally. At some point you have to let it go and move on to the next sale. One of the best words is *next*. I would say next out loud, then clap my hands to wipe off the fatal dust and get ready for the next prospect.

Don't pay interest to something that won't bear a good return. Many times salespeople will allow the past to manipulate their day. They spend the day reliving their lost sale until it destroys their faith and robs them of their confidence. Don't allow the past to control your future because it is costly. Hit the delete button and move on. The world's greatest closers let it go and get their game face on for the next opportunity.

Salespeople who don't close beat themselves up with their self-talk when they lose a sale. The result is deadly to income. Talk yourself up, don't beat yourself up. Your self-talk really determines who you are; it determines your self-worth and image. Words are powerful and when you strengthen your vocabulary you will also strengthen your mind. The two go hand in hand.

Words that will tear you up:

- I should have.
- I blew it.
- What an idiot I am.
- Why wasn't I prepared?
- That prospect is a jerk.
- I am so weak at times.
- I wish I were better.
- I hate my job.
- That was such a waste.
- What a fool I am.
- Why can't I be better?

- I'm going to look for another job.
- Selling is tough.
- I'm so stupid.
- I hate this.
- I can't last much longer doing this.
- I am going to start sending out resumes as soon as I get home.
- This business is not for me.
- Why is that guy a natural born salesperson.
- Why do I have to work so hard at this.
- I don't care, I'm not going to be here much longer anyway.
- I can always go back to my old job.
- I wish they had trained me.
- It seems like I can't get a break.
- That customer was a jerk.
- I am so dumb.
- Why is this job so hard?
- When does it get easy?
- I'm gonna quit this.
- I hope my old job will take me back.
- Everybody wants it for nothing.

Do you see how the above sayings can damage your confidence? Which one have you caught yourself saying? When you catch yourself saying it, stop and say something like, "I didn't get them this time, but next time I will! *Next!*" Move on. Let it go.

Paying attention to a lost sale will rob you of these world's greatest closer tips:

1. Game Face
2. Positive Mental Attitude
3. Confidence

4. Self-Worth
5. Enthusiasm
6. Will-to-win
7. Proper use of selling scripts
8. Proper selling process
9. Persuasion
10. Passion to close

Sales is a game of no and yes. You should be prepared to hear yes but in fact, you should prepare to hear the word no. Since 80% of most sales are made after the fifth time you ask for the order, it doesn't make sense to be afraid of the word no. No is two thirds of yes. It's a letter away. If you have played sports then you know that there are certain consequences in sports. If you play football, then you can expect to get hit. If you play softball, then you know the ball will get by you eventually. If you swim, you know you will get wet ,and if you don't paddle, then you drown. If you play hockey, you are going to get hit in some form. In sales, which is like a sport, then you know you are going to lose

and most likely it will be to the word no. It doesn't make sense to let it ruin your day. Let it go, say next, move on, and get your game face on before you face the next prospect.

Are they saying no to me or no to my product?

Most of the time your prospect is saying no to your services or your products. They are saying no to the performance, not the performer. You can't take every loss personally. If you did your job and you asked for the order then most likely your prospect is saying no to your product. The more prepared you are for the presentation and the skills needed to overcome the objections, the easier the close will become. Think about how many salespeople have come and gone in your organization over the last few years. A third of most sales teams turn over because the salespeople didn't make it. Years ago, sales managers would often be heard saying, we need to hire four so one can make it. That's 25% make it, and 75% don't.

If you want to become more focused in life and sales, then simplify your life by doing less and getting more done. Multitasking is a disease. Salespeople attempt to do too many things at one time. With social networking growing, Internet surfing now a work sport, when do people have time to work? Before you know it the day is over, and soon the month. Do less and get more done. If you find yourself putting things off, there are several reasons. One could be you don't know how, you don't like it, you don't see the value, or you aren't going to be there long. If you want to get something done, just get up and do it. Speak up and say, do it now, do it now, do it now. Write it out and keep it in front of you.

ASK AND YOU SHALL RECEIVE!

CHAPTER ELEVEN

Close the Deal

Serve, then sell

- The world's greatest closer knows when to break out the commission breath and close like a champion. The weak salesperson tries to close way too early in the process. If you want to close more sales do this:
- Give more than expected. Inch by inch it's a cinch, by the yard it's hard. Always go the extra mile and you will see extra profits.
- Use your prospect's name throughout your presentation.
- Remember important facts, dates, company history.
- Prepare like a champion so that you can fight like a champion when you are selling.
- Serve people first. We are in a service business, not serve-us.
- Tell the truth at all times, it only takes one lie to be a liar, if you are good, you won't need to lie. If you are weak and don't have true selling skills, then most will lie.

- Wow your customer by outdoing your competition. Do the little things, follow up with a call, send a letter, email, or text.
- Know thy product, please. Know what you are selling how to present it with enthusiasm. Years ago *USA Today* said the number one death of salespeople was their lack of product knowledge.
- Don't be pushy with your prospects; there is a difference between being pushy and being persistent.
- Don't be afraid of asking for the order. You deserve to ask if you have followed the selling process.
- Keep your prospect involved by asking questions that keep them personally involved.
- Don't BS your way through the sale. Prospects can usually pick up when manure is being spread.
- Don't use words or phrases that sound like you are lying. "Well, to be honest with you..." I always come back with, "Why, were you going to be dishonest?"
- Don't approach your customers with greetings like this: Can I help you? Do you have any questions? I bet you want one of those, don't you? Are you prepared to do something today or buy today? These are weak openers.
- Always take the high road when talking about your competition. Don't badmouth them or the salesperson you are up against. If your prospect feels that way, it doesn't mean you have to feel that way. Overcome it by saying, "I'm sorry to hear that. However, let me show you why you would want to purchase or consider our product."
- Use power words like: best, incredible, unbelievable, prove, outstanding, advantages, benefits, level above all, special, can't miss, league of its own, can't measure the value of it, priceless, leading edge—which is better than cutting edge—can't live without this.

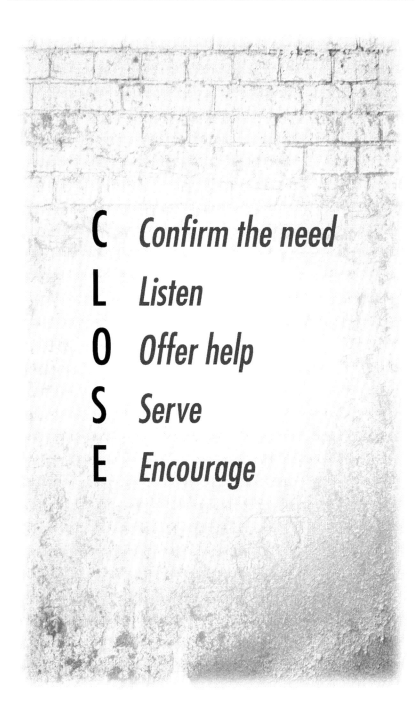

C *Confirm the need*

L *Listen*

O *Offer help*

S *Serve*

E *Encourage*

- Give more than you're paid to do. Most salespeople only give enough to make a sale. Most of the time you will fail with that attitude. Give more than expected, whether you get paid of it or not. Whatever you throw out in life, is what you get back most of the time, so if you throw out just a bit of effort, passion, or persuasion, then please only expect to get back what you give out.
- Always be closing yourself and your customer. Think of your sale this way, If you aren't totally convinced of your product and that you think you can close the prospect in front of you, then most likely you will be able to improve your closing ratio.
- Never take the word *no* personally during the sale, get past it, go past it, get around it. No means your prospect doesn't *know* enough to say yes right now.
- Make a friend first, then sell your product or services. People don't like strangers. Make a friend, earn a sale.
- Close—Lose—Closing—Losing—Closer—Loser

C — Confirm needs
L — Lead to benefits they care about
O — Offer solutions
S — Serve then sell
E — Encourage your prospect do buy right now

Close the sale: Now comes the easy part of the sale. Yes, I did type that. Let me type it again: here comes the easy part of the sale. You ask for the order. You close or you lose. When closing your sale, do your best to use a choice question or an either-or question. Give your customer two choices. It can be as simple as this:

Salesperson: "Well, should we schedule the install date on Monday or Wednesday?" Or "I have the paper work right here, are you going to be the only one on the contract or will your partner be on there, too?" Or, "Thanks so much for your help, let's get this wrapped up right now, will you be you be purchasing with cash or a credit card? Which address do you want us to use, your home or work address?"

The close is the easy part. The world's greatest closer is never afraid to ask for the order or the sale. **Just close it!**

To be the world's greatest closer, it will take all of your being—soul, heart, and mind must be in sync.

The World's Greatest Closes

Closing isn't where you take a big breath, cross your fingers and eyes, and then turn into a mealy-mouthed, below-average, weak salesperson who couldn't close a door with a hurricane behind them. Closing is just another step of the sale. What you have to remember is that your customers will feel nervous when making decisions. If you have followed the basics of selling, then closing is just another step. It's just another question, and you have to remember that.

Fear is ignorance. Fear is cured by knowledge, which is powerful when placed into action. You can't let fear stand in your way or you won't ever progress. Fear can be overcome with practice. Fear is the darkroom where people develop the negatives in their life. The world's greatest closers use fear as fuel to propel them to ask and close the sale. You have to move to what you desire, not what you fear. If you have twenty closes in your toolbox—which is called your vocabulary—you will never be afraid to close your sale. If you don't close, you lose; if you aren't always closing, you are losing. If you aren't a closer, you are loser, and by that I mean you will lose your sale, your commission, your attitude, your referrals, your repeat business, and soon your job.

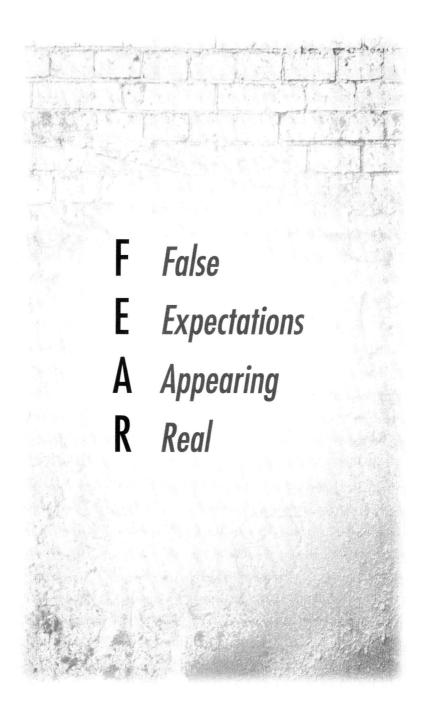

F *False*

E *Expectations*

A *Appearing*

R *Real*

Twelve Closes to Help You Close More Sales Right Now

1. Summary close:

Three minor commitments, positive sentences, either/or closing question "Well, Mr. and Mrs. Smith, you both see the value in the product, don't you?"

"Wouldn't it make your life a lot easier?"

"Isn't it going to be great to be able to use this around the home or office?"

"It really sounds like we found the right equipment for you. Are you going to pay by check or credit card?"

"Would you like us to start the installation on Monday or Tuesday?"

2. Same price close:

There will be several times when you hear your prospect give you this objection.

Customer: "We really like your product. However, we don't make snap decisions, so what we would like to do is compare your prices with your competitor just to make sure we are making a great business decision."

Use the same price close with this customer. "If our price was the same as their price, who would you rather purchase from?"

If they say you, then go for the close by saying, "Great, let's get this wrapped up. By the way, did you want us to ship that overnight or go with regular freight?"

3. First place close:

This is a great close when your prospect gives you this age-old objection.

Prospect: "Just to let you know, we never buy at the first place we shop at."

Salesperson: "Let me ask you a question. All joking aside, if you lost your car keys at home, and you found them in the first place you looked, would you keep looking?

Prospect: "Of course not!"

Salesperson: "Great, let's get you guys signed. Are you going to pay by credit card or check?"

4. You only live once close:

I love this close, it's a great close to use on a customer who really loves your product but they think they can't afford it.

Prospect: "We just can't afford it, it's just too much money for us."

Salesperson: "I understand, but you do see the need for the product, don't you? Why not get what you really deserve? You only live once. Plus, I bet you have both worked hard, haven't you? Why not get what you really deserve? Did you want to put that on your credit card or will you be writing a check? Come on, folk,s let's quit putting life on layaway and start enjoying life right now!"

5. If you were me close:

The prospect can't make up their mind; turn it around by saying this.

Salesperson: "Okay, I understand that you want to a make a good decision, as most people want to do. By the way, if you were me, the salesperson, and you had a customer who wouldn't buy, what would you do to get them to buy today?"

Prospect: "I would drop the price!"

Salesperson: "Okay, great, so if I can get you to agree on the price, is there any other reason why we couldn't wrap it up right now?"

6. Success on layaway close:

Prospect: "We just can't make up our mind and we are going to hold off for a while."

Salesperson: "I understand, but you do like the product, don't you?

Let me ask you a question. Aren't you tired of putting life on layaway? Why not start living today and enjoying your new widget today? I'm so proud of you folks, did you want to use a debit card or will you be paying cash?"

7. Pressure close:

Prospect: "I think we better be going, you are starting to put too much pressure on us."

Salesperson: "I understand, I just don't want you to mistake pressure for my enthusiasm, it's just that I love helping people and selling our products. I mean, you do like the widget, don't you? Plus it will make your life a lot easier, won't it? So let's take care of the minor details and get you guys on your way home with your new widget."

8. Final figures close:

Prospect: "Our company really likes your product and services, but as we told you earlier, we need to be at this price, because that is what we have budgeted for this purchase."

Salesperson: "Okay, I completely understand. However, you did see how the product could save you money and increase your products, didn't you? So if we could agree on the final figures, is there any other reason why we couldn't wrap this up right now? Let's come to an agreeable figure is that fair enough."

9. Ben Franklin close:

Prospect: "We just can't seem to figure this out and we need to really take some time and think about it before we make a decision."

Salesperson: "I understand and before you leave, why don't I give you some information that you can take home and review? Is that fair enough?

Have your prospect sit down and take out a sheet of paper and draw a picture like this:

Yes	No
Like color	*Price*
Right size	
Like ease of use	
Comfortable	
Economical	
Time saver	
Warranty	

The goal of the Ben Franklin close is to get your prospect to agree on what they like about your product and to sum up the selling process. Each time you get a yes, put a checkmark next to what they like. Then when you get at least six to eight yeses, look at your prospect and hand them your pen and say, "Mrs. Prospect, if there one thing stopping you from making the best decision, what is it? Here take my pen and please write it out for me." The objective is to get your customer to flush out the objection. Once it comes out, then you handle and overcome it. You could come back with this: "Mrs. Prospect, other than the price is there any other reason why we couldn't get this wrapped up right now?"

10. Are you saying no to me close:

Prospect: "I just can't make up my mind."

Salesperson: "I understand, but are you saying no to me, or saying no to the price? Let's work it out because it sounds like you want to make sure you are making a good decision, am I right? Why put life on layaway? You only live once, so let's get you taken care of. By the way, do you want the payment to start on the first or fifth of the month?"

11. Silence must mean yes:

How many times have you heard that when you ask for the order, you are to shut up? That's true to a degree, but if you ask for the order and they don't say something, you have to come back with an answer. After asking for the order, there is a pause. You want to wait for your customer to respond to your closing question. If they don't respond in a short time, say, "Mr. Prospect, I have heard that silence means yes, Is that right? Great, congratulations, do you want to take delivery now, and how did you want to pay for it—check, credit, or cash?"

12. One to ten close:

This is a great close to flush out the objection and then be able to close on it.

Prospect: "We aren't really sure."

Salesperson: "Oh, I understand. Let me ask you a question. On a scale of one to ten, ten being the best, how would you rate our product and services?"

Prospect: "It's about a seven."

Salesperson: "Okay, that sounds fair. What would make it a ten then?"

Prospect: "Well, the price is a bit too high for me."

Salesperson: "Okay, if we can fit the price in your budget, is there any other reason why we couldn't wrap it up right now?"

Now obviously you can't use every close for every situation No close works every time. Like a master technician, you have to have all types of tools, and at some time, you will reach down and use the tool. There is no bag of trick closes. Each close has its own personality and after you practice the closes, you will be able to use them with ease.

You will begin to notice that after a while, the closes flow naturally, because you have practiced them until they become part of your everyday vocabulary. When the closes work without any real work, don't look at your customer like "I can't believe this worked." Just go with the flow. Remember, closing isn't one big breath with a mousy, whiny voice saying, "What do you guys think?" Closing is a process that starts taking form in the first minute of being in front of your prospect.

I repeat: nothing is acquired without practice, sweat, frustration, hopelessness, moments of excitement, and the guts to keep practicing your scripts. Commit your scripts to memory so you don't have to play the *I guess and I hope* game. Read your closes out loud, write them down on three-by-five cards, review, and role-play them until you can say all twelve closes in row. It can be done. I have twenty-five closes committed to my memory and anytime I'm called on, I can recite them.

CHAPTER TWELVE

Working Toward Career Goals

Green Berets and how they relate to your becoming a Great Closer.

I have admired the Green Berets for years, and while researching this book, I found out some interesting information that will make sense to you in your development to become a great closer. Green Berets react to situations with expert thinking and skills to handle just about any situation. They require over eighty weeks of training before they are placed in action. It can come down to life or death. Selling is not life or death but there is success or failure. Most salespeople don't get eighty weeks of training. Most get desk, a territory, watch some old videos, follow the old guy, and "Hurry up and get out there and make us proud."

"That's all they pay me!" No—that's all you're worth! I should be paid more—No, you should sell more! I can't get a break—You can if you make your breaks! I don't get house deals, only the house mouse does. Yes, most businesses have a mouse house. It's nice to get a freebie now and then, but you don't want to depend on house deals, because your skills will erode and when the spoon-fed deals stop, you starve.

You need skills to pay the bills. If you think that you will become a top salesperson with below-average skills, then you might need to hit your refresh button. Your paycheck is determined by your skills and your vocabulary. If you don't practice, then you won't ever be able to execute effectively.

What are words worth? In the English language there are roughly 450,000 words. Eighty percent of most people's vocabulary comes down to about 450 words or less. If you want to earn more money, then you will need to expand your vocabulary. Look at *Readers Digest*—for years they have had a section called "Enrich Your Word Power." If you expand your vocabulary then you will expand your income.

Practice, Practice, Practice

What else is new? If you cheat on your practice, you will be found out at the end of the month by the size of your paycheck. You can't go around blaming anybody but the person in the mirror you face every day. On the way to work, you practice, on the way to a meeting, you practice. It's okay to practice on breaks.

Go Through Life — Or *Grow* Through Life

Most salespeople will just go through life, you want to grow through life. Why is that? If you grow your skills, you will grow your income. If you don't slow down, then you won't be able to speed up. You have to constantly sharpen your skills. When they get dull, that's when you get in a rut, which is a grave.

Will Hard Work Make Me Rich?

I wish it would, because that would mean everyone who worked hard would be rich. How many of us know people who worked hard and still don't have two pennies to rub together? You soon look at these good, hardworking people and find out they have worked hard for some twenty to twenty-five years and barely have a few thousand dollars in savings. Soon they will be on a fixed income. Have you ever noticed that most people who are on a fixed income are broke?

Now, I am not saying that hard work won't help you. I just wouldn't bank on it to carry you to your goals. I will say this, though— don't be afraid to work hard. Throw effort at your work and it will pay you back. The lack of work will kill a man, but hard work won't.

Why not work SMART?—Specific, Measurable, Achievable, Realistic, Timely

Work smart not hard—an old saying. But how do I do that? Follow my recipe!

- Show up to work with your game face on every day. Focus, and channel enthusiasm.
- Listen to self help CDs or podcasts everyday on the way to work.
- Close the first customer and the last customer of the week.
- Don't listen to negaholics who tell you why you can't, instead of why you can.
- Work like every day is the last day of the month.
- Set a few daily goals, keep your list in front of you, and review throughout the day.
- Develop a mastermind group of professionals who will help you, not beat you up with excuses.

Experience Versus Everyday Improvement

I don't know how many times I have heard salespeople tell me that they have forgotten more than I will ever learn. Have you ever heard that before? Typically there are three types of people in a sales department.

The human sponges. They soak up every bit of information they hear. It seems like they are in a constant mode of improvement. You tell them something or send them to workshops and they take notes like they are in college again. They review, write, practice, and implement their new skills.

Vacationers. This group of salespeople make me laugh, they just want a free trip to the top. They belong to several social clubs at work. If you send them to training or place them in training, they are more interested in what's for lunch than what they will learn. The WFL—What's For Lunch—group does exist in a lot of businesses. They actually spend more time planning their lunch than planning their day.

Prisoners of life. This group exists in almost every sales organization. I have done hundreds of speeches, keynotes, and seminars. As I get ready for my shows, I tend to give thanks for the ability to do what I love to do: help people improve or get through their struggles. A prisoner typically shows up with a ball and chain attached to their leg. They are forced to come to training. Typically they are know-it-alls. They will tell you about their experience and brag about how many years they have been in the business. Yawn.

Be wary of this bunch because they are the low-hanging fruit who have bruised egos and negative attitudes. They are the energy thieves of life and work. It's going to be tough to reach the top while the bottom is trying to pull you down. Sales is a very competitive market. You would think as you are climbing to the top, that others would applaud your effort and results. It's normally the opposite. Most people don't want to see others succeed, because it makes them transparent—it shows their faults or their truths. Most people would rather run from the truth instead of facing the truth. One of my favorite quotes is " The quicker you come to truth, the less pain you have to go through." Just be honest with yourself.

Excuses why salespeople fail

They fly around like the air we breathe, don't they. The world's greatest closers don't use excuses to make themselves feel good. They don't sugarcoat the reasons they fail. If you don't close, you lose, if you aren't closing, then you are losing, if you aren't a closer, then you are a loser. It's blunt but truthful, isn't it? Life is black and white and the faster that you accept that, the more sales you are going to close. If you aren't in a constant state of *creating*, then you are in a state of *disintegrating*.

The Professional Excusiologist list

1. Management won't work with me.
2. I can't get a house deal.
3. All the best leads go to Sammy Spoon.
4. I can't get a break.
5. They gave me the worst territory.
6. The top guys have been here way too long.
7. Nobody likes me.
8. They won't talk to me.
9. I can't get a break.
10. It's the wrong time of the year.
11. Business is bad all over.
12. The economy sucks.
13. Our product is old and outdated.
14. Our service sucks.

15. Our commissions got cut.

16. I'll get 'em next month.

17. Why did that person get ahead of me?

18. Management is pathetic.

19. I'm only in this for a bit longer.

20. I can't get anybody to work with me here.

21. Traffic is bad, I can't believe I missed my appointment.

22. Whatever.

23. It's the wrong month.

If you aren't gunning for the top spot, then what are you aiming for? Have you ever heard the statement that second place is first place for losers? Why would you aim for anything less than the top? You can climb any mountain if you are properly equipped and have the right frame of mind. The quicker you come to truth, the faster you will be able to race to your goals.

If you want to be the world's greatest closer, I can tell you the one person who can help you the most isn't the person you see in the mirror every day. You need not look any further. You must break free of your comfort zone and the anchors that are holding you back. Most likely it's the past that stops you from going forward.

Selling Triangle and How To Build Value Through Winning Presentations

Present — Convince — Persuade — Close

The presentation is where the emotions of the buyer are rising and where they become excited about you, your product, and your company. The presentation is when you, your product, and company are on stage. It's a show and though a lot of salespeople have the talent to sell, they lack confidence. There really isn't such thing as a natural-born salesperson. The key to a winning presentation is to combine your words, tone, inflection, and body language in sync, sort of like the rock group NSync. All the moves, music, and words were choreographed.

Most people fear public speaking like death, because they aren't prepared to stand and deliver an Oscar-winning presentation. If you know your product, have the right words in place, and feel comfortable, then your presentations will be unbelievably fired-up, which will result in increased sales. That's what the world's greatest closers do. They create a selling atmosphere, where energy is flying with enthusiasm as its fuel, to help you close your sale. When you put it all together, the close is easy. You have to get your prospect so excited about you, your product, and your company that they can't say no to you. Now that's a closer.

Your entire goal for the presentation is to wow them and to get them to believe that they can't live without you, your product, and your company. Here are some of my best tips to being a champion presenter:

World's Greatest Closer Tips To Help You Close More Sales

- LAST—Lasting Attitudes Sound Terrific
- Image
- Eye contact
- Smile
- Put prospect at ease
- Connect with customers or prospect
- Serve your customers, then sell them
- Become more interested than interesting
- Visual aids
- Facts
- Trial closes using yes questions—tie downs
- Vary your tone and inflection

- Make your presentation interactive
- Ask questions to receive feedback
- Listen for buying questions
- Use Feature Advantage Benefit (FAB) selling
- Direct audience participation
- Impact selling presentations
- Make it fun
- Verbal input back from your prospects
- Prospect involvement
- Proof book

Mastering selling skills

If you build your sale on sand it will fall apart. If you build your sale on lies it will blow up in your face. If you build your sales on truth you will become the world's greatest closer. Don't try to be a fast talker or pathetically weak and drop the price the moment you meet a prospect. Of course everybody wants a good deal, don't they? Isn't a good deal a product they can love at a price they can afford from a salesperson who will take care of them after the sale?

Building a sale is like building a home. You need land, plans, material, and a foundation. All have to be in sequence to build a home. A sale isn't any different; there has to be a foundation in place or the sale will crumble like a cookie.

Definition of the word BUILD!

Everyone wants to succeed and create a lifestyle that allows them live a better life. Most salespeople want to know the tricks or secrets of the business. It would be better to learn the craft so that you can craft your sale. Mastering how to *build* your sale will improve your closing ratio immediately.

B—Brief: Keeping your presentation *brief* will keep your prospect involved and interesting. If you are all over the place, talking too much, soon your presentation will be boring and outright horrible. Build your sale on the key motives that excite your prospect.

U—Uninterrupted: A champion closer doesn't take calls, send emails or text messages, or take smoke breaks. Once you are perform-. ing your presentation, you have to keep yourself and prospect focused. If that concentration is broken, then most likely you will have to start over. Once your sales momentum is broken, most likely you will be broke, too.

I—Interactive: Keeping your prospects involved is so important today since most prospects shop through their computer, text most of the time, and rarely communicate verbally anymore. The best way to keep your prospect involved is to ask quality open-ended questions. Get your prospect involved with their five senses. Get them to touch, smell, feel, look, taste what you are selling and the value will rise like a cake in the oven.

L—Lead to the benefits that they care about and desire. If you do that, you will be able to stay connected with your customer. Present the benefits in a pattern where you are providing solutions to their problems. People do buy products; however, they need solutions to solve their problems. This is true for any type of industry. People don't go to the dentist for fun, they go there so that the dentist can help them through their problems or prevent future problems from coming up. If you present solutions, they will be more likely to buy.

D—Developing urgency is vital to closing your sale, if you decide to forgo talking about urgency throughout the sale and then try to bank on it to close your sale, your prospect will feel like they are being pressured or lied to and will bring up objections.

If you follow the above recipe for success, your closing ratio will improve.

Proper Practice Prevents Poor Performance!

As I was writing this book, I happened to be doing some consulting for a large retail business. After being there for two days, a salesperson came up to me and said, "Can you help me out?" He told me that he was with prospects and could I come over and talk to them. He apologized to me for putting me on the spot. I said I'm not on the spot, I'm always prepared for the sale no matter where I am. You can develop into that too. The poor below-average salesperson didn't have the skills to slow the customer down. Follow the basics, and you can control the selling process and soon the customer will follow you. It's too easy.

I was out on the lake in my kayak on a Saturday afternoon. A woman yelled out, that is a nice kayak. I responded, "Yes, it is nice, isn't it?" She said yes. "How much was it?" I said, "It really depends on the options you pick out. Would you consider a two-seater, or a one-seater?" She said, "Two-seater."

You can get to this place, too, no matter where you are. If somebody asks how much is it, you can respond like the world's greatest closer. The scripts won't sound like scripts if you practice them, as I just showed you. Practice is about sweating and perfecting. When you get in the game of selling and closing, there is no need to sweat if you practiced like a pro. The Navy Seals have a great quote, "The more you sweat in practice, the less you bleed in battle."

How Do I Master The Words?

Learning something new isn't always the easiest thing to do. Most salespeople don't want to take the time to develop their selling skills, so they get stuck with the skills that they possess. They get frustrated when they don't improve and tend to blame the circumstance rather than the person in they see in the mirror. Learning skills is an art, and I can tell you, like any sport you have ever played, it does take patience, practice,

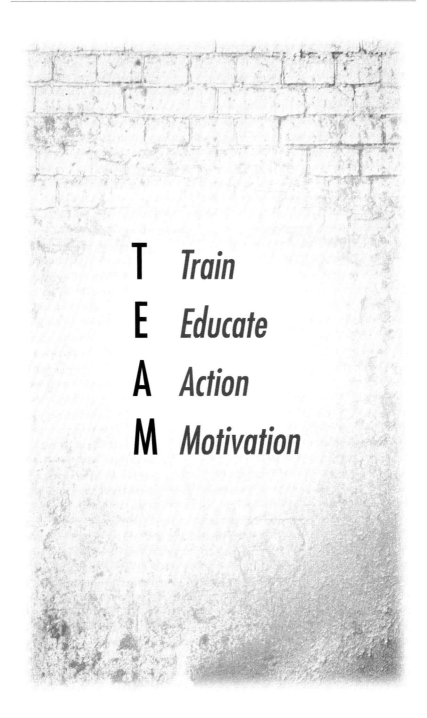

T Train

E Educate

A Action

M Motivation

and persistence. Don't worry if you make mistakes, because the world will forgive you if you make them, but it will punish you if you hold back. You are what you think and you will hit what you aim for and in sales it comes down to the words you use and how you use them.

Teach me the tricks

I have spoken to thousands of people and have told them repeatedly that there aren't any tricks of the trade. Master the trade and then you won't need tricks. As with a sport, it takes time to build a muscle and in sales, your tongue is your muscle. Be careful—it is in a wet spot and it tends to slip quite often.

How to memorize scripts — William Powell's four levels of thinking.

In 1937, William Powell discovered the four levels of thinking and if you follow his thinking and my ways of practicing your word tracts you will soon master the art of selling.

Four Levels of consciousness.

1. Unconscious incompetence—You don't know really what you are saying; you respond with whatever words you think up on the spot.
2. Conscious incompetence—You know what to say but you repeatedly make the same mistakes and know you make them.
3. Conscious competence—You know what to say but when put on the spot you have to think about what you are going to say. Salespeople who hesitate normally lose sales. "If you think, you stink."

4. Unconscious competence—This is the highest level of thinking. I have it and have worked to achieve it. The world's greatest closers have this level of thinking. When they are put on the spot or hear an objection, they respond without having to think about what they are going to say. Tiger Woods has it, Michael Jordan has it, I have it, Wayne Gretzky has it. You can get it, too.

How do I master the Script? Practice — Practice — Practice

Why is that on a Sunday afternoon as you flipping through the TV channels do you see these event occur? Tiger Woods taking a birdie putt on eighteen from forty feet out and making it! Kobe Bryant making the last shot as the clock shows two seconds left. Michael Phelps winning eight gold medals at the Olympics. Have you ever noticed the ESPN Sports Center only shows the highlights?

Sitting back in your La-Z-boy, you think, Boy, that was lucky! You then get somewhat motivated and run outside and no matter how many times you shoot the ball, you can't hit the side of a barn. You putt a hundred times and after missing a hundred you say, this ball won't work with me or something of the sort. It happens like that every day for most people. It's because they don't want to practice. If you get one thing out of this book get this right here: Practice until you get it and then use it.

Flash Cards

I have mentioned the use of flash cards earlier; they are very effective. Three-by-five index cards will work well. Write out your script. Take the script out several times a day and read it over and over until you don't need the flash card anymore. Learning new scripts also takes a few more ways to master them. Do it this way:

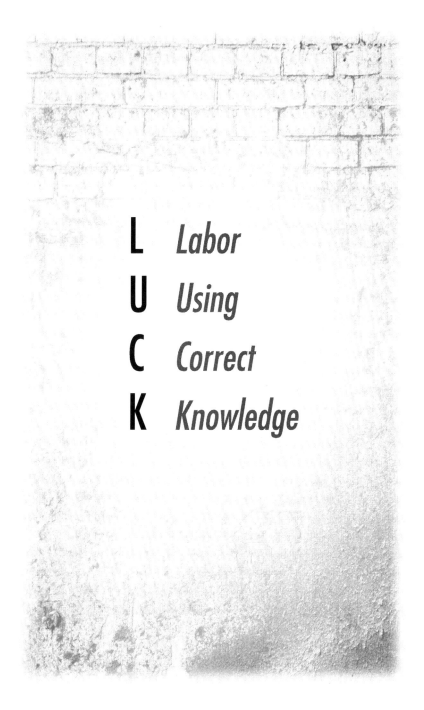

L   *Labor*

U   *Using*

C   *Correct*

K   *Knowledge*

1. Write the script out thirty times.
2. Read the script out loud thirty times.
3. Record the script word for word with a voice recorder or video camera.
4. Listen to the script thirty times and role-play it.

When I was hired to be a speaker trainer for a large sales training organization, I can remember them telling me that in this job you must be perfect from day one and then improve from there. Talk about pressure. I attended several of their seminars which were two to three days long. I would sit in the back and I would take notes throughout the day. No matter how many times I attended the seminar, I would always write out the same thing over and over. If I had attended the show thirty times, I had thirty pages of the same words, quotes, and scripts. I would then type them out and place the important scripts on flash cards. There was an estimated twenty hours of speaking for the three-day show. I know that it took me over one hundred hours of practice to master one hour. Do that math on that one!

The difference between you and me and the others is that you and I will pay the price for success. It's called practice! Take the time every day to improve your scripts and the returns will be great.

This is the most powerful method to master a script, you hear it, you say it, you write it, and your record it. It will take time just as it takes time to build anything in life. Look at an oak tree—it takes years. Muscle building takes times. The problem today is that nobody wants to take the time to learn anymore. Today's society has become a one-click download generation, and if they can't get it fast enough they click off the site and go on to the next site. Great salespeople know it takes time to develop and use their new skills. Look at any sports player and you will find out the years it takes them to reach the major level. How many people hit the big time without practicing?

Self Discipline and What It Means to Me

Self-discipline starts when lip service stops. Self-discipline is all about training and developing your skills; it will mold, correct, and straighten out your words and your habits. It will help you become a great closer because you paid the price in practice.

Clarity brings focus—My definition of focus is:

F — Faithfully
O — On
C — Course
U — Until
S — Sold or successful

Clarity removes chaos and doubt. If you know exactly what to do each selling day, then your day will be productive and will end in great results. Don't ever accuse busyness for productivity. The world's greatest closers major in major objectives and goals, not in trivial minor activities. The world's greatest closers know that their purpose is what fuels their passion for living and selling. You can feel it miles away, can't you? When you walk into the world's greatest closer's personal circle, you can feel their energy. It's contagious and something you want to catch. They have a glow around them, their face is lit up, their smile is warm, and their handshake is friendly.

BTNA- That means Big Talk No Action

Have you ever met that person? All talk no action. Self-discipline comes in a few different colors such as: Put your money where your mouth is. Talk is cheap, your actions speak louder than your words. Self-discipline is doing something without being told. Start off improving your self-discipline by doing one activity you have been putting off. You will get overwhelmed if you attempt to do too many activities at one time.

Goals — The further you start back in life, the more control you have over your future.

George's ten Best Ways to Reach your goals

1. Visualize your goals – you must see them before you can achieve them – Write them down, Mark Victor Hansen says, to write out 101 goals – Don't forget 94% of written goals are achieved.
2. Goals must be purpose driven. Your purpose must be bigger than your goal!
3. Goals must be specific and measurable.
4. Stretch yourself out of your comfort zone. You can't change being comfortable
5. If you don't succeed, find out why and then adapt and adjust.
6. You don't have to know how to get to your goal, just know that you will.
7. Keep your feet moving towards your dreams. Don't wait until the last day to take one big step.
8. Take one step to success each day, not every other day.
9. Goals are backed with faith, effort and belief in self. The greatest of all is faith
10. Never give up, let up or shut up until you reach your goals. You live once and die forever, so go for it!

Magic comes to life

Goals are like magic. They take you to desired places. If you set a goal to become the world's greatest closer, it can happen. Goals to have to be realistic and achievable. The deadliest sin of goals is setting your goals too low and actually hitting that target. You have to put your goals out of reach. Most people go through life with meaningless goals and wake up one day and wonder where their life went. Time is your enemy.

There are several types of goals and several levels of goals. It doesn't matter what industry you work in, or the place, the goal is to be the best at whatever you do, whether it's working at a fast-food restaurant, hospital, factory, in the sales profession or a service business. The world's best closers work in different types of industries. There are always certain goals that can be met. However, no matter the profession, you must always strive to be the best. Setting goals, and making a plan to reach your goals, will help you in every area of your life.

The 3-10-87 rule — Where your wealth becomes a predictable result

Studies have shown that only 3% of the people who set goals actually reach them. Proof is what happens to people when they set their New Year's resolutions. In fact some 80% of people who set New Year's resolutions fail by January 31. Ten percent of most people set goals but lose interest and give up on the way to their goals. That means that only 3% of the people who set goals actually reach them. You don't have to know how to get to your goal, you just need to know you will reach your goal.

The world's greatest closers set goals and then write a plan out on how to achieve their goals. They ask big questions such as:

1. Who will help me on my way to my goals?
2. What prospects do I need to spend more time with?
3. Why do I want to achieve my goals?
4. When do I get started on my path to my goals?

5. What happens if I don't change?
6. What new material or personal development do I need to help reach my goals?
7. Do I need to take time out for personal and professional improvement?
8. What bad habits do I need to break to get to my goals?
9. What is my purpose to reaching my goals?
10. Who will I help to reach their goals so I can reach my goals?

Most salespeople try to figure out everything before they start their journey to their destination. It's okay to see the end today. People fail at the start of their goal-setting because they think of the cost of getting there. Today's generation has been built on *I need it by yesterday*, because *now* is too late. There is a process that has to be followed on the way to your goal. Don't worry about the cost of getting to your goal, or like a dieter, you will say, "Oh, the pain is far too much for me to endure." Or the person who wants to start an exercise programs says, "Oh, the pain is too much, I have to get up early, the weights are heavy, I have to give up my favorite foods." These people are the masters of start-and-stop programs.

Three Powerful Words

When you set your goals, be careful of the words you use. These words can destroy any chances of you reaching your goals.

Weak Words That Need to Be Eliminated

1. I want to
2. I can't
3. I'll try

The World's Greatest Closer's Words

1. I'm going to
2. I can
3. I will

Wanna Bes or Gonna Bes: The world's greatest closers are going to be, not want to be. Your self-talk will determine the height of your goals. If you are wishy-washy, your goals will be the same way. These are the words you need to be successful:

1. Decide
2. Commit
3. Succeed
4. Win

You want to have goals, but more important, you're going to reach your goals. If you don't have a starting point, then you will end up being lost. The results are tragic. Goal-oriented salespeople have to have a starting point. Without a starting point or a clear purpose and goal, your foundation for reaching your goals will be weak and feeble. A few bad days will literally knock you down, and before you know it, you will be saying, "This month is shot, but I will get 'em next month." The daily choices you make will be based on pressures, deadlines, stress, and your feelings at the moment. The end result is that you will try to do too much in too little time, and that causes stress, fatigue, sales burnout, and eventually the death of a salesman.

If you are going to hit your goals, then set them right now. Sit in a quiet place, close your eyes, and start imagining where you want to be in your personal and professional life. Don't worry about the cost of getting there or the work you have to put in to get there. Take out a pad of paper, and as fast as you can, start writing down your goals. Don't stop writing. If you put a jet or a battleship, that's okay for now. Imagination and creation are born from the same mother, they go hand-in-hand. If you aren't in a state of creation, then most likely you are in a state of disintegration.

Prioritize Your Goals

Once you have written out your goals, you need to prioritize them. This will help you line up what you need to attain first or where you need to place your focus. It's like a magnifying glass. Once you shine the light on an objective, the beam, which is small but focused, generates heat.

The Power of one, two, three.

Your ability to reach your goals can be improved if you number them. For example, a **number one** is a *must* goal for you right now. That could be a certain income, number of activities, a certain account you are going after, personal improvement, diet, maintaining your energy, better home life, and so on.

Number two goals are bigger goals and might take you a bit longer to reach, because you want your goals to be realistic and achievable. The timeline might be longer and the cost to get there a bit more expensive. For example: top salesperson, most deals closed in a month, highest gross income, most prospects seen in a month, hardest worker in company, and along the way you set some personal goals, income goals, family goals, or health goals.

Number three goals are somewhat out of this world, but that's okay. It could be to own the company, have a net worth of millions, a yacht, passive income, a jet, a home in Hawaii... The dates might be a bit longer but it's still okay to dream big.

Knowing Your Goals

It will define your position in life and your career. It will set apart what you accomplish and what you won't accomplish. The further you start back in your life the more control you will have over your future. Sales is the same way, If you want to be at the top, then you have to set goals today and then place coordinated activities in motion and monitor them.

Failure can't be an option for the World's Greatest Closer

The road to success is paved with daily victories and failures. Don't ever look back, because you won't be able to go forward. If you think that the career you are in is not for you, then you will start looking back. When things get tough, you get tough, when things aren't going your way, change, adapt, adjust, and attack.

Rolling University

Think about all the time you spend in your car if you are a traveling salesperson. The hours are crazy, aren't they? If you spend an average of two hours a day in your car and multiply that times five days times 4.5 weeks, times twelve months that comes out to 540 hours spent in your

car. I did the math—that means you are in your car for over 13.5 work weeks over the year. Did you know that it takes about 250 hours to obtain a masters degree? Why not use your car as your rolling university? Listen to self-help programs or programs on selling so that you can develop yourself into the world's greatest closer.

The benefits will bring you more income, satisfaction, and for some, job security. Selling will actually become easier. Many people in my seminars say, "Oh, I wish that selling was easier." I answer, "I just wish you were better." Start developing the habit of listening to self-help programs on developing a positive attitude so that you are prepared to sell and close. Like going to the gym, you might not see the results today; however, in time, your closing ratio will improve. The key is not to hold onto success too long, because contentment will come along. Have you ever said, "Oh, I remember when I used to do that?"

Develop Multiple Sources of Prospects

The top producers in sales know that the most profitable groups of prospects to sell to are the prospects they have already done business with. The results are huge when you follow up with customers that you have already sold to. The profits are bigger, with bigger commissions. Plus, who wants to sell to strangers, anyway? People like to buy from people they know, trust, like, and believe. That is why it's hard to get new accounts sometimes. The prospect you are attempting to sell probably feels very comfortable with the person that is their sales rep. That prospect normally will pay even more for the product just because they like their salesperson. As the saying goes, "No like, no sale."

You can win more if you follow up with your sold and working customers. It's that simple, but for some strange reason, salespeople treat follow-up like punishment. Only the weak-minded think like that. The world's greatest closers are not afraid to follow up and don't give up. If you don't follow up, you will kill your career on the installment plan. It's as useless as blowing up a balloon that has a hole in it.

Consistency is the key to follow-up — don't give up but follow up

If you follow up consistently then you will be able to predict your sales future. If you don't follow up consistently then you will be left at the mercy of your selling climate. In other words, when it's hot, it's good, but once it cools down, that's when you are left out in the cold. The results can be fatal to your career.

Follow-up is like farming. There are similarities. Most farmers know that to grow a crop of corn it takes about ninety days. The farmer has an accountable partner to report to: Mother Nature. If the farmer lives where the seasons change they must plan their crops according to the seasons. That means the farmer can't run out in the month of October and throw the corn seed down and say, "Okay, now, let's hurry up and grow." Too late. And in sales, most salespeople are too late. They work the market when it is hot, as you should; however, when that market dries up, you will be left at the mercy of the market. In sales that means there will be several ups and downs or peaks and valleys.

Become A Management-Driven Salesperson — The Beginning Of The Next Sale

The sooner you start with follow-up the more control you have over your future, which means you will be able to predict your sales and income. Follow-up will help you if you are organized. Insuring a long-term sales career takes commitment, backed with organized effort.

Selling is like a wheel; the key to a long-term career is to keep that wheel spinning. If you don't touch the wheel, then it won't spin, and the cycle is broken. Think of it like this: when you sell your prospect they're at the top of the wheel. Visualize them heading down now. You've sold them and that sale is over. The buying cycle has three components to it. Cold—Warm—Hot. In the buying cycle you would now say that prospect is cold. They aren't hot anymore because they have bought. With a systematic follow-up plan, the goal is to bring them back to warm again and then move them to hot. When they are hot, that means they are ready to buy again.

In some cases the cycle can be a short time. In other businesses it could take years to bring them to the hot status again. Now do you see why you need to follow up consistently? I can tell you this, I have bought a lot of products in my lifetime, and I would be lucky if I had a few companies or salespeople following up with me.

There are really only two ways you run you career.

You can either be linear or residual-driven. They are completely opposite.

Linear

The definition of linear is a straight line. That means whatever way the market goes, you go with it. If it's a great market, you will enjoy it and be able to capitalize of it. However, when the market goes down, you go down with it. This is obvious—salespeople get fired for lack of production because they were at the mercy of the market. Most of these salespeople are defined as the go-with-the-flow type. They march with the economy, and follow-up, for the most part, is put on a layaway plan. They are selling with the market, and they aren't preparing their pipeline. They will tell you that they don't have the time; too busy selling, working long hours, have to capitalize on the market while it is hot, and the excuses go on.

Now, I am not saying that you should not jump on the market when it's hot. Capitalize on opportunity. However, keep following up, marketing, planting seeds, prospecting, calling lost prospects, lost sales, mailing, and driving your follow-up activities. I can tell you this, I have never seen a market stay hot forever. Selling is cycle driven and as good as it is when it's hot, it can be equally cold. A look at 2008–2009 will back up that fact.

Residual Management Driven

This is how the world's greatest closers run their career. They know that follow-up and prospecting will insure long-term success. This is a close buying, term insurance policy. As long as you pay for the premium you are insured. When you quit paying, you are left uninsured. That means you are linear-driven again. Oh, and forget about customer loyalty. That has been placed in a museum of the past. The definition of residual selling is a salesperson or company placing activities in motion today to guarantee sales down the road. Whether it's blogging, emailing, texting, phone calls, mail, visiting clients, sending letters, marketing, getting your face out to your customers, or advertising, all of these have to be in sync to insure long-term success. Do this and you will never be at the mercy of the market.

Even if the economy goes down to new lows, your hit won't be as drastic as everyone else's, because you were planting seeds for the next sale. The best part of all is that the prospects you have sold before want to buy from you again and the commissions you make are normally bigger. Doesn't it make sense to grow your business instead of just going through business?

Gaze into My Crystal Ball

What a myth it is that if you gaze into a crystal ball you can see your future. You can see your future today if you placed activities in motion today. It's almost Biblical. The good book says, "As ye sow, so shall ye reap." Follow-up is the same isn't it? Why is that we have to go back thousands of years to confirm what works? Companies and salespeople are always looking for the new way of selling or the latest gimmick to sell more. Technology has changed and has become more automated, which will allow you to be more efficient and profitable. However it all goes for naught if you don't do it!

The follow-up Process: Essential to Your Continued Success

1. It should be systematic, meaning that the follow-up process is done the same way every time.
2. It should generate consistent, predictable results.
3. It should require minimal physical interaction to make it run, meaning it should be able to run on autopilot. That is why CRM software is needed.

I once had a salesperson tell me that she liked to handwrite follow-up letters to all of her customers. I agree the personal touch is best; however, when you have hundreds or thousands of prospects in your database, automation is useful. Automation will leave you more time to do what you do best, sell and close sales.

The death of follow-up occurs when salespeople aren't organized. When asked to follow up, they take it like someone is force-feeding them medicine. The secret to follow up is to be organized. Sounds too easy, doesn't it? If you work too much in your business then your business will suffer. You must also work *on* your business along with working *in* your business. You have to balance it.

Follow Up—Don't Give Up.

There are several different ways to follow up, as well as different types of customers that you should follow up with.

1. Sold Prospects—you have already sold them
2. Usual Prospects—these are working prospects
3. Target Prospects—people who are in your marketplace looking for your product or services

1. Sold Prospects: Sold prospects are pretty easy to follow up with, because you have already earned their trust. The walls have come tumbling down, so make a warm and fuzzy call to check in and see how things are going. Crazy as it sounds, most likely you will stumble into a sale while doing this. Always ask for referrals from this group. They like you, so they will want to help you. I was speaking for a $9.5 billion trade association and was doing some prep work on the phone. The person who brought me in gave me two huge referrals in another state.

Get up with the times!

The most effective way to follow up is by visiting your prospects in person. However, that is not always possible, since some of your prospects might live on the other side of the world. The fastest way to follow up today is by email, text messaging, live chat, and so on. Time is precious and you have to use it wisely. (Time is money, too.) The key is to set up your database so you are reaching your customer in a way that people respond to. Today most people are contacted by email or some sort of technology. If you aren't there yet, you better hurry. **Developing multiple methods of contact will bring you multiple sources of prospects. Reach your prospects through:**

1. Email
2. In person
3. Phone
4. Direct mail
5. Texting
6. Trade shows
7. Advertising
8. Referrals
9. Networking

10. Web presence, search engine
11. Social networking
12. Marketing materials

Follow-up has to be in sync, ongoing, and never-ending. Once you break the chain or consistency of follow-up, your competitor will step in and you will be long forgotten. It could take up to twenty-one times of consistent follow-up before your prospect responds to you in some cases.

Customer Loyalty

Forget about customer loyalty if you don't follow up. I am sure you will have a small group of sold prospects ask for you, but think about how many times you have sold a product or service to a customer who came back to buy again and didn't ask for you. The reason they don't ask for you is because you didn't follow up. Less than 10% of salespeople follow up. Don't give up—follow up, and you won't have any competition. If you are loyal to your customer, there is a good chance they will be loyal to you.

2. **Usual Prospects:** The customer who has left without buying your product or the prospect you have left without a sale is a hot prospect. The reason for this is that they haven't been closed and they have unspent money or funds ready to be spent. Speedy follow up is needed as they are nearing the end of their buying cycle. They are going to buy soon. It comes down to this: **Who is going to sell them? When are they are going to buy?**

I hope you are the answer to the above questions. Follow up is the key to you building your business. Follow up accordingly:

- After the appointment, call them and thank them regardless of whether they bought.

- Send them an email or text.
- Follow up with a personal handwritten note.
- Set a follow up call or visit.
- Make yourself available to them and easy to reach.
- Tell them to call you if they have any questions about what you are selling or even your competitor's products.
- Be a resource for them; let them know you have more to offer than the product you are selling.
- Place them on your email database follow-up system.
- Send them a newsletter or a special-occasion print letter.
- Just do it!

3. Target Prospects: No matter what type of sales you are in, you are always searching and rescuing new prospects. They could include places you spend money, visit, clubs you belong to, trade shows you attend, referrals you are seeking, trade associations, lost prospects or suspects, and just about any other place you can find suspects.

Suspects Become Prospects Then Sold Customers

Obviously the hardest type of person to follow up with is a suspect, because they don't like you. Or they might not know about you or your product. The closing ratio with this customer is very low. Your job is to move them through the buying cycle. Some will buy and some won't buy, and that is the attitude you have to take with these prospects.

The world's greatest closer doesn't accept mediocrity. Prospecting is lot like digging for gold. Lots of digging and soon you hit a nugget or a vein. The problem for most salespeople is that they like the gold, but not the work to find the gold. So their database isn't being mined. Crazy, isn't it, that salespeople won't work their database?

I was hired as a consultant by a business that was losing sales. Their advertising, marketing, and cost of business was going up, and sales were going down. I get paid for one thing: to tell the truth. It's brutal at times for me to tell the truth.

This sales organization had several thousands of sold prospects in their database. The best way to insulate your business from the volatility of the market is to protect the customers you have already sold to. It makes complete sense, doesn't it? Less than 20% of the sales force did proper follow up. That means that the other 80% of the sales force didn't, wouldn't, couldn't, and won't follow up. I asked the company how long they had this problem. They said forever. I asked them, "Why won't they follow up?" The managers said the salespeople just wouldn't do it. Every time I hear that, I think that those salespeople are the best, because they've sold their managers on not doing follow up.

Your database is your gold mine, your insurance policy, your future, your life, your higher profits, your best way to reduce your advertising and marketing costs, your best chance of reducing employee turnover, and your best way to have a long life in business and sales. If you don't work your database, your competition will. You won't notice it at first. The leak is minor and most businesses patch it up with excuses. You can hear them now, can't you? You call up your weak management like this: "Jonesy, please come up to my office. I need to know what is going on with our sales. I want answers, what is going on?"

"Well, to tell you the truth," Jonesy, the weak manager who can't get the salespeople to follow up, says, "I have called around and checked with other companies like ours and they are having the same problems as us, boss. I also have been watching the news and they are painting a grim picture, too, plus last year at this time, boss, we were going through the same cycle."

Isn't that about the time, the CEO comes back with things like this: "Jonesy, if I wanted to hear excuses, I could find them anywhere. I don't give a hoot about the other guys in our business. Why don't you really tell me the truth, why aren't we selling more?"

"Okay, I will tell you, but don't fire me. I can't get the salespeople to follow up and take care of their customers."

"Jonesy, I see the problem here."

"Oh, that's great, boss, what is it?"

"Jonesey, you can work, but you just can't work here anymore."

There are several great speakers out there who speak on leadership and the development of leadership. It all comes down to common sense. You have expectations and standard operating procedures. You train your team, hold them accountable, and have a pay plan that rewards above-average performers. Those who fall short will have to leave because you don't have room for people who won't follow, can't do, don't want to do, or won't ever do. How hard can that be? Look at the word LEADerSHIP. Why do you think that the word Lead is front of ship? You lead from the front.

If you are a business owner, corporation, or salesperson, you have to realize that some people aren't ever going to do follow-up. You have to pick your battles and fight the ones you can win, and with the other battles, you need to find a way to get it done by doing something different. If you are a parent then you know exactly what I am saying. You don't fire your kids because they don't get straight *A*s, do you? Salespeople are the same way. If they aren't going to protect your database, then it's up to you to find a way to get it done. Firing everybody who doesn't do it may be not the answer. If you don't want to do it, then find another way to get it done. Just get it done!

An Easy Ten Ways to Follow Up With Suspects and Prospects

1. Don't be afraid to do it.

2. Take immediate action when following up. Always offer something to them that is a benefit.
3. Pick up the phone and call them right now.
4. Find out when you can get belly-to-belly with them again.
5. Know when to let go of your prospect—*Quit* beating a dead horse; it's dead.
6. Offer solutions to them.
7. Rinse your commission breath.
8. Send a follow-up personal note.
9. Give more then you expected to give. The little things make a huge difference.
10. Just do it.

How do I Improve My Closing Ratios Today?

The best way to improve your closing ratios is to track them through planning and then understanding where your best customers reside. The best customers who will bring you higher closing ratios are the ones you have already sold to. In sales there are two sides to a career. You will be on the left side of sales or the right side. You don't want to stay on the left side because it will bring you little money and tons of frustration. I have met so many salespeople who took up a full-time residence on the left side.

It doesn't matter how large an audience I speak to, I can see them nodding at me with the pain of regret on their faces. Thinking to themselves, "I should have moved over to the right side. Oh, how miserable I am to be still working hard and not being rewarded for my efforts." The fastest way to move to the right side is to commit to your career. It all starts by being decisive and then moving from a job to a career. I once ran into a salesperson who challenged me and said, "Yeah, but the left side develops character." Okay, no problem, you can do that if you want. However, a rewarding, fun sales career is all about working with the most profitable, fun, easy-to-close, pay-me-the-most customers.

Job	Career
Cold Prospects	Repeat Customers
Hard To Sell To	Fun to Deal With
Typically Small Commissions	Bigger Commissions
Longer Sales Cycle	Shorter Sales Cycle
Good For Short Term Success	Long Term Success
Least Productive	Most Productive
Low Closing Ratios	Higher Closing Ratios
Doesn't Follow Up	Follow Up System In Place

Let me ask you a question. What is the problem with common sense? You're right—it's not common. Where do you think most sales-people spend their time? The right side or left side? Most spend it on the right side. However, if you are a true professional, you are on the right side of sales or heading there. Now do you see why you have to commit to a career?

I once heard a speaker say that a lot of people are looking for the rosebushes without realizing the rosebushes might be out your front window. The best career might be the one you have right now. Seize it and go for it. The payback of follow-up will reward you forever. The answer is to have *multiple sources of prospects* so that you can insure a long-term sales career. That way, if some of your sources of prospects dry up, you will have several more to sell to. Don't put all your money in one bank. Spread it out so that you are balanced right.

CHAPTER THIRTEEN

World's Greatest Closer's Tips

1. Have an attitude of gratitude everyday.
2. Wake up to your favorite music.
3. Preplan your day before you start your day.
4. Ask yourself: who is going to help me, how long will it take, when will I start?
5. Practice pays dividends. Use your car as your rolling university on the way to work for self-improvement.
6. Minimize negativity and shoot all negaholics with positive statements.
7. Prioritize your activities so that your day doesn't plan you.
8. Write out five small goals each day, even if they are the same goals each day.
9. Keep your goals in front of you at all times.
10. Always ask this question during the day: Am I doing the most productive activity that is leading me to a sale right now?

World's Greatest Closer's Fifty Bonus Tips/Quick reminders

1. Seventy percent of prospects buy because they like, trust, and respect you.
2. Serve, then Sell—Serve your customer first then sell them.
3. Let it go—don't let regret control your day—WGCs don't sit and pout over their losses.
4. Solve problems—sell solutions.
5. PPPPP—Proper Planning Prevents Poor Performance.
6. No lack allowed. Losing Attitudes Can Kill.
7. Follow the basics of selling be a salesperson in control.
8. Common ground allows you to build rapport with your customer. If they don't like you, they won't buy from you.
9. Shortcuts are pay cuts—if you skip steps, you skip sales.
10. Luck selling—The word LUCK means – Labor Under Correct Knowledge.
11. If you don't close, you lose.
12. Don't chase false objections; develop the skills to overcome objections. No means not now, tell me more so I can say yes.
13. Selling Triangle—WGC knows they have to sell themselves, their product, and the company.
14. Practice your selling skills everyday—You are in the everyday business of selling. Practice ten to fifteen minutes a day.
15. Stick to the script or you slip. Sales is all about word tracts, role-play your scripts until they sound natural.
16. "I wish selling were easy or I wish I were better." Practice your craft so you can craft your sales.
17. Use positive thinking to get positive results. Talk yourself up instead of talking down to yourself. Good in, good out.
18. Self-help, or Shelf-help—take time to study and read up on

current selling trends. Take ten to fifteen minutes a day to read and refresh your selling skills.

19. Use your car as a rolling university. Over the course of a year, if you drive two hours each day to work, you will be in your car over 540 hours. Use that time to grow personally and professionally.

20. Go to work and work. Don't go to work to break, and kill time. You can earn more money right now by showing up to work with a plan and then working your plan.

21. Improve your production by improving your energy. Fast food and energy drinks are fads and Band-Aids. Take care of your body. Eat right and work out so that you can be more productive.

22. Respond to failure with optimism. Winston Churchill said, "Winning is maintaining your enthusiasm while you're losing." Typically in sales you will hear more nos then yeses.

23. Turn your job into a career—*job* means Just Over Broke, a job is what you work at, a career is what you develop.

24. Goals—keep your goals in front of you, so you can maintain enthusiasm. The further back you start in your life, the more control you have over your future.

25. Don't give up but follow up. Forty-four percent of salespeople quit after making their first call. If you follow up, then you won't have any competition.

26. Persistence eliminates resistance. Studies have shown that 80% of sales are made after the fifth time you ask for the order.

27. Know the product. Study your product until you are so convinced by it that you would buy it. If you don't know your product, then you won't have the enthusiasm to convince your customer to buy it.

28. One more call—when the day is ending don't let up or give up. Make that one extra call.

29. Build value in your product or services throughout the sale.

Prospects buy when the value of owning your product is greater than owning your price.

30. Manage your activities daily so you don't have to wait until the end of the month to crush it. Professionals know every day where they are with their selling activities.

31. Just close it. Nike says, "Just do it"—same thing. Just close it. Ask for the order or someone else will. The worse thing that can happen is that they will say no.

32. Don't leave messages on voice mail. They just get deleted. The reason they don't call back is because you don't create excitement and give them a reason to call back! Leave a short enthusiastic message. Not some boring, long, below-average message that gets deleted before the entire message was heard.

33. Rinse your commission breath—prospects like to be helped and then sold.

34. How to last in sales—The word LAST is defined as Look-Act-Sound-Think like a professional. Shoes shined with a brick aren't a good first impression, dress up to go up in sales.

35. Be Bold and Courageous—Have the guts to ask for the order. When you look back, you will have regrets because you didn't ask for the order.

36. WGC knows that selling is convincing their prospect, and convincing is persuading prospects to buy now. The word NOW means—No Opportunity Wasted.

37. Networking is far better than not working—Spend quality time letting people know who you are, what you do, and where you work.

38. Eliminate the word try from your vocabulary—The word try has a built in future for excuses- replace the word try, with I Will.

39. Turn your Setbacks into Comebacks—All closers will fail at some point in their sales career. Life allows you to make U-Turns.

40. Don't give up after a bad first half of the month. Quitters never win, and Winners never quit. Too often sales people say, "Well this month is shot, I'll get them next month."

41. Don't quit. When in doubt throw effort and faith at doubt and fall forward.

42. Build value in yourself, your product and your place where you work at. That is called the selling triangle. Like a fire, it takes three components to build a fire: heat, oxygen, and fuel. Remove any one of them, and the fire goes out. Selling is the same way: sell yourself, your product, and the place you work, and watch your sales rise dramatically.

43. Close a sale on Friday, so that you can carry it forward to Monday. Don't get on the Friday afternoon bus looking forward to the weekend, as most salespeople do. Make that one extra call, visit, or presentation. The weekend, not Friday afternoon, is for winding down.

44. Be wary of energy thieves whom you might work with. With sales being so competitive, be careful of people who do their best to steal your energy by getting you caught up in the backdraft suction of gossip and backstabbing.

45. Manage your own energy so you can manage your own paycheck. You have one body, so why not take care of it? Selling isn't physical, it is mental.

46. Take care of your body, eat healthfully, and have your energy moments of the day preplanned. There is nothing worse than a salesperson who spends more time figuring out what's for lunch than what their selling game plan is for the day!

47. When calling prospects, get right to the point; say this: "Let me get right to point of why I am calling. I am calling to let you know..."

48. If you can't give 100% today, at least give 50%, and from there

give 100% of the 50% so that you can have a productive day, personally and professionally.

49. FACE—Focused And Channeled Energy. Have your game face on while selling.

50. Just *do* it!

CHAPTER FOURTEEN

Now What Do I Do?

By now you are probably fired up like a six-pack of Monster. To leave where you are, you need to ask yourself some big questions. Your life is a road paved with successes and failures. No matter where you go, no matter who you are with, no matter where you work, there will always be things you enjoy and things that you won't enjoy. That's life, and life is what happens to you when you least expect it. The world's greatest closer isn't so much about closing deals or making money. It's more about doing the things that you might have put on layaway. Success won't fall unto your lap unless you're in the right place at the right time. Even then you have to get there by some chance. Success in life is different for each person. One person might think that just having a few bucks in their pocket is good enough. For others it might be the giant mansion and millions of dollars. For me, it's helping every person I meet. That's good enough for me. I have never chased money, but I have chased my love—helping people live a better life at home and work. Life gives you one chance. Why wait for things to be perfect?

Don't put your life on layaway. If you can commit to your decision, then most likely you won't be stopped. For you to be successful, you have to live in harmony with your heart, brain, and soul in sync. Your body is a machine, and it needs a maintenance program like any other machine. You have to take time to read so that you can keep improving your mind. Taking time out to work out will keep you physically fit. One of your goals is to undertake the task of living in harmony where your heart, soul, and mind are connected.

You can get to your goals faster if you take time to write your specific goals and then place a timeline on it. If you write it and don't place a date or time, then it will surely fall into the I-will-get-to-it-tomorrow basket. The real character of a person shows over time or after repeated failures. You will be meeting challenges every day, and it is easier to give up sometimes than it is to get up and get going again. Life is more about the comebacks than the setbacks. The world loves to hear rags-to-riches stories, doesn't it? No matter how you fall or where you fall, whether it's in your personal or professional life, at some point you have to get up, and put that right foot in front of the left foot and start marching towards your dreams and goals.

I will never forget my father telling me when I was a young boy that everybody gets their turn in life. I didn't quite know what he meant, but as I grew up and went through some personal and professional failures, I understood what he was saying. There will always be tough times in life. Failure is when you give up. The climb up from failure begins with one step as you repeat the words, "I will never give up, let up, or shut up until I am called up." If you give your best to live and your best to sell, nothing can stop you from becoming the world's greatest closer.

The world's greatest closer can sell anything to anyone as long as they have complete belief in self and product. Confidence comes to you from repeated victories and loss of faith comes to you in the darkness of night when you are lying by yourself and you start asking questions. "Can I do this?" Doubt creeps in and pushes your faith out of your mind.

If you got this far in life, you are a winner. As a matter of fact, the day you were born, you were a winner. The odds of even making it to birth are a miracle. The best part of life is that you can always leave behind what you don't want to carry forward. The so-called baggage of your failures should be put out on the curb today for the garbage man to haul away. The hang-ups you have can be hung up, too. Easier said than done, though. Most people in life have three things: hurts, habits, and hang-ups. The past is past and can never come back physically, but it can mentally. Your habits, which started out as your friends, may well become your masters. Your habits will surely determine your future. As for your hang-ups, maybe it's time today to let them go as well. Most of these were caused by someone in your past. Most likely they have long forgotten what they have done to you, and yet you let them hurt you. Let it go and move on.

Most people go shopping for a way to improve their lives. They are called fad shoppers. Whatever is in style or new, people run right out and buy it, hoping it will improve their life. Most of those fads have a short shelf life. Most likely they are unhappy people always looking for something to fill their void. I have seen people chase things—fast cars, expensive cars, jets, vacation homes, businesses, yachts, plus more. They can't buy enough happiness. None of those will buy long-term happiness because that can't be bought. Sadly, they are desperate, lonely people looking for something they will never find.

Your purpose in life is to serve others. That is the sole purpose of your life. You can read all the self-help books in the world, but the one book that you will always come back to is the Bible. It by far is the number one self-help book in the world. The Good Book is like a blueprint of how you should live your life. If you ever fall into darkness, run to the Good Book and you will find your answers to your questions. Vices such as pills, drugs, or any other mind-altering influences are nothing but Band-Aids. There is nothing more powerful to help you improve in life than the development of your knowledge through education. I once heard that you will learn 75% of what you need to know in life after the age of forty. Show me a reader, and I will show you a leader. The last thing you want to do is spin your wheels in life and then look back and find out you made a lot of noise but didn't get any farther in life and your career.

Change is hard. At some point it may be better to pull out what has been put in your life. Most people know what to do, but they can't figure out why they don't do it. The world's greatest closers know what to do and just do it—and so shall you. They don't need pain in order to change. They leverage their mind and say, "If I stay here it will cost me more than the cost to change. So I am going to change, and I will profit from my change."

Closing the sale is easy as long as the groundwork has been properly prepared. The close is just another step and it actually becomes a minor detail. It doesn't matter what you sell, either. Closing is easy as long as you followed the basics. The road to the sale which has been around forever is paved with the basics. Follow them and they will lead you right to the bank.

Self-help or shelf-help

Often you will see people buy books like this or DVDs and back of the room products sold at seminars. Hopefully you won't be the person who buys the material and then proudly places on their shelf-help book case. If you buy then apply it.

I am encouraged to see people take action and look forward to improving their lives. I was speaking at a seminar and one person told me this, "What a shame it is for the people to buy all that stuff." I said, "Why is that?" He said, "Well for one thing almost everybody who buys it won't listen to it or do anything with it." That might be the way he sees life. I don't see it that way. I am the World's Greatest Closer and my mission in life is to help everyone I meet improve their lives. When I speak at my seminars my goal is to inspire everyone to take action when they leave the seminar.

Human beings are in a race that we each win at some time. Some of the people's races will be short while others will endure for quite a long time. That race will bring you to the end of your life. I can't tell you how many people I know who didn't get to be here for a long race. Someday that race will end for you, and there will be a knock at your door. The question will be asked, "Do you have any regrets?" Most people will regret more of what they didn't do than what they did. What were they waiting for? Why did they put life on layaway?

Don't wait until things are perfect to move on. Do it now!

ASK AND YOU
SHALL RECEIVE!

APPENDIX

Acronyms

LACK — Losing Attitudes Can Kill

ATTITUDE — A T T I T U D E = 100%

COACH — Convince Over Achieve Care Help

TEAM — Truth Everyday Always Matters *or* Train Educate Act Motivate

FACE — Focus And Channeled Enthusiasm

BUILD — Brief Un-interrupted Interactive Listen Develop

CLOSE — Confirm Listen Offer Serve Encourage

BASIC — Be A Salesperson In Control

WFL — What's For Lunch

NFL — Not For Long

FNG — Fabulous New Guy (or Girl)

NOW — No Opportunity Wasted

WIN — What's Important Now

SIASM — See I Am So Motivated

GAME — Give All My Enthusiasm

DARE — Describe Act Roleplay Encourage

SAND — Stand Around Not Doing

LUCK — Labor Under Correct Knowledge

FEAR — Forget Everything And Run
GOYA — Get Off Your Ass
BTNA — Big Talk No Action
SOYA — Sitting On Your Ass
JDI — just do it
JCI — Just close it
TPD — Think Plan Do
CASH Career - Attitude - Skills - Habits
KASH — Knowledge - Ability - Skills - Hope
FEAR — Forget Everything And Run from fear and chase education, it reduces
     ignorance
SWAT — sell what's available today
TIPS — to insure performance salesperson
ASK — Always - Seek - Knowledge

Made in the USA
Lexington, KY
28 October 2019